FAILING TO WIN

MIKE QUINN

Enjoy the ride—
and don't be
afraid to fail!
Mike

FAILING TO WIN

HARD-EARNED LESSONS FROM A PURPOSE-DRIVEN STARTUP

MIKE QUINN

"This raw, honest account is a must-read for anyone thinking about starting a company and for every entrepreneur who feels alone in the journey."
Elizabeth Yin, Co-Founder and General Partner of Hustle Fund

"Far too often we focus on startup success stories – but you will learn so much from Mike's tale of 'failure.' His honest and vulnerable story of entrepreneurship in Africa reveals just how much failing is baked into the foundations of winning, along with a healthy dose of tenacity and the absence of bad luck."
Michael Jordaan, Venture Capitalist and former CEO of FNB

"You learn more from failure than from success. This story is a gift for entrepreneurs and indeed anyone wanting to learn about the first generation of African fintechs that paved the way for future companies to thrive. A golden thread runs through every chapter and phrase of *Failing To Win*: the reason and mission behind Mike's work, his why. I cannot wait for the next chapter in his unfolding journey. This book is a must-read for all entrepreneurs wanting to do something on the continent."
Katlego Maphai, Co-Founder and CEO of Yoco

"Mike's purpose-driven journey with Zoona is filled with so many incredible lessons for anyone who is seeking to build a high-impact venture at scale in Africa. The tenacity, resilience, the highs and the lows highlight how failure is a critical building block of innovation. It proves that in life it's those moments when you are willing to go where no one has ever gone before that will define you and propel you to win."
Marlon Parker, Founder of RLabs

"Startups are hard. Startups in Africa can be really hard. Most people understand this. However, most people don't understand why. Mike's story is a rare glimpse into how challenges present themselves – and ultimately how to overcome."
Matt Flannery, Co-Founder of Kiva and Branch

"From their first transaction in 2009 to reaching millions of unbanked and underserved people, Zoona's overall impact on financial inclusion across Southern Africa cannot be understated. However, what's even more remarkable are the untold stories that made the Zoona vision a reality. In a rare look behind the scenes, Mike Quinn shares a vivid picture of the other side of leadership we don't talk about enough. As he aptly describes 'founding, failing and winning', this book highlights the risk of taking that all-important first step, embracing failure and ensuring you learn the transformative lessons critical to success as an entrepreneurial leader. I would highly recommend this book as a quick study for mission-driven people who aspire to impact the lives of others and move from success to significance."
Fred Swaniker, Founder of African Leadership Group

"Innovation has gone global, and is transforming people's lives around the world. But startups are risky. Sometimes they scale and sometimes they fail. In *Failing To Win*, Mike shares insightful lessons from his journey at Zoona about what it takes to operate with integrity, impact and inspiration on the new Frontier of Innovation."
Alex Lazarow, Global Venture Capitalist and Author of
Out-Innovate: How global entrepreneurs – from Delhi to Detroit
– are rewriting the rules of Silicon Valley

"For anyone wanting intimate knowledge of how to do business in Africa, *Failing To Win* is a must-read. From start to finish, you get a first-hand, no holds-barred testimony from a genuine entrepreneur on what it means to do business in Africa. Thank you, Mike, for your honesty and courage and sharing what so many of us navigating the African business landscape need to learn – and that is 'failure is a stepping stone to greater glory.'"

Dr Rutendo Hwindingwi, "The African Realist", Business Development Leader Deloitte Africa and Emerging Markets

"I have known Mike as a fellow entrepreneur in Africa for the last decade. I was inspired by the team culture of performance and family he built at Zoona and I remember vividly visiting their HQ and thinking I wanted to re-create this in my own company. Mike's humility, resilience and depth of knowledge of how to build a pan-African business are unique, and his testimony of experience is an important short history of the fintech boom on the continent."

Elizabeth Rossiello, Founder & CEO of AZA

"This book is about so much more than failing (in order) to win. It is real. It is laced with inspiring stories of women like Misozi and Sandra, who shared Mike's commitment to purpose with profit. With head, heart and soul, Mike invites us to journey with a founder/entrepreneur-turned-CEO, time and again snatching victory from the jaws of defeat right until the very end. We face the angst of engaging faceless corporates that shapeshift unpredictably. Above all, this book is about people, but also about passion, purpose, courage and growth."

Dr Ndidi Nnoli-Edozien, Investor and former Chief Sustainability & Governance Officer of Dangote

"I read *Failing To Win* in one sitting. It is a pacey, well-written account with real lessons for building a purpose-driven business in Africa, and filled with personal emotion and excitement. I highly recommend reading it!"

GG Alcock, Author of *Third Word Child,*
KasiNomics* and *KasiNomic Revolution

"*Failing To Win* is a captivating account of an incredibly talented and unusually forthright entrepreneur who built an ambitious purpose-led company that started in Zambia. The venture defied many common beliefs about what cannot be done, it empowered customers and employees alike, and it unleashed the 'fintech revolution' in one of the less likely parts of Africa. Mike Quinn lucidly explains all the highs and lows, without falling into the two polar traps of either ignoring the failures or letting them define the entire experience. At Oxford I have taught the Zoona case study to countless MBA students to show how fundamental principles of entrepreneurship can be meaningfully applied in a novel context. It just takes courageous and smart individuals who are not afraid of failing (in order) to win."

Thomas Hellmann, DP World Professor of Entrepreneurship and Innovation at Saïd Business School, Oxford University

"Startup life is a rollercoaster. Sometimes your best day and worst day can be the same day. Mike shares his entrepreneurial story that transcends borders and provides important insights to founders on the journey of building a company."

Brian Requarth, Co-Founder of Viva Real and Lattitud,
Author of *Viva The Entrepreneur: Founding, scaling,*
and raising venture capital in Latin America

ABOUT THE AUTHOR

Mike Quinn was co-founder and CEO of Zoona. He is now CEO of Boost, which he co-founded to enable informal small businesses to thrive in Africa's emerging digital economy. Mike's entrepreneurial journey in Africa started as a volunteer in Ghana and Zambia with Engineers Without Borders Canada. He has received a Skoll Scholarship for Social Entrepreneurship from Oxford's Saïd Business School, the Edward W Claugus Award for Leadership and Innovation in Financial Inclusion from Accion, and a Social Entrepreneur of the Year award from the Schwab Foundation.

•
This POD edition printed, bound and distributed by Amazon
www.amazon.com
•
Also available as an ebook and audiobook
•
Originally published in paperback in Southern Africa in 2021
by Mercury, an imprint of Burnet Media
www.burnetmedia.co.za

To Isabelle:
As Louis de Bernières predicted,
our roots have so entwined together
that it is inconceivable that we should ever part.

CONTENTS

PART 3: WINNING

PROLOGUE

APRIL FOOLS'

April Fools' Day, 2019 was no joke for me or for the 127 employees of Zoona, the African fintech company I had co-founded a decade before.

Ironically, it was the tenth anniversary of Zoona's inaugural transaction — that moment in 2009 when we took the first step toward our long-term vision of "a cashless Africa." We had no shortage of ambition then, believing this was the beginning of our startup dream to create a billion-dollar business, the coveted "unicorn" status promoted by Silicon Valley as the bar for entrepreneurial nirvana. We wanted more than that, though: Our company would be known as much for its positive impact as for its commercial success.

Ten years later, the message I delivered to my staff was a world apart from that original vision. I was announcing the news that most of them would be out of a job in the coming weeks and months, and that I too would be exiting from a company that had become intertwined with my identity. It certainly wasn't the ten-year milestone celebration I had envisioned — especially since we had been on the cusp, just ten months earlier, of closing a landmark $40-million Series C investment round, which would have launched Zoona toward becoming a multi-country digital bank on the leading edge of Africa's emerging financial technology (fintech) ecosystem.

April 1, 2019 was a painful moment of truth for me, capping a dramatic week.

For the previous few years, my partners, my board and everyone else at Zoona had looked to me, as the CEO, to solve our recurring and always urgent cash-flow problems by finding yet more investment capital. Indeed, that was my duty and obligation. But by late March 2019 it had become clear that our current crisis had developed into an unprecedented existential threat to the business. As I lay awake in bed one Sunday night, I realized I couldn't prevent the thing I had most wanted to avoid and had been most afraid of for all those years: Failing.

The next morning, I called my co-founding partners Brad and Brett Magrath into our boardroom, and we drew the curtains on the windows facing the hallway, a warning signal to passing staff that all was not well. Behind me was a wall of quotes from our investors about why they loved Zoona and had staked tens of millions on us. I could tell from Brad and Brett's bloodshot eyes that they hadn't slept any more than I had.

I laid out our plan. Brett and I would resign and Brad would take over as CEO. We would lay off all of our headquarters staff, except for a handful of people to keep our transaction engine and call center going. With revenues still flowing from our subsidiaries in Zambia and Malawi, we just might be able to avoid driving over the cliff in the next few weeks. There would be no April salaries or severance packages for any of the people who had given so much of themselves to Zoona, simply because we didn't have any money to pay them. The best we could do, in lieu of a package, was create another liability on our insolvent balance sheet in case Zoona could ever be resurrected in the future.

I set up an emergency call with our board to lay out the grim details, which I knew would come as a shock. The board had come to expect that we would find a solution to the latest challenge and soldier on, as we had done so many times before — after the Zambian currency imploded, after our expansion strategy failed, after the $40-million investment round collapsed. Every time, we'd rallied from the brink of failure because my partners and I refused to quit, exhibiting a tenacity that enabled us to build a pioneering fintech business that directly improved the financial well-being of millions of consumers, created thousands of jobs and built a globally recognized brand in two African markets on nobody's radar.

But this time was different. We were out of options, and I could see no way for the company to survive with me at the helm — or even still in it.

The board call was beyond somber. Tears were shed, more for the loss of a dream and good people than for my departure. Everyone accepted that for me to stay on as CEO was not in the best interest of the business. I apologized because I rightly felt the weight of the responsibility: We had failed to win.

* * *

I walked out the door that day questioning all the decisions I had made for a decade, questioning whether success for a startup like ours in Africa was even possible — and wondering if I were a failure, too.

This book started as a way for me to answer those questions; as a letter to myself, looking back over a decade of my life to understand what really happened. I needed to come to terms with how radically different the ending was from what I had expected, or at least what I had hoped, it would be.

As I wrote, I started to see in hindsight not just what went wrong, but how: Mistakes in judgement, overconfidence in some decisions, a lack of confidence in others, and sometimes just bad luck or bad timing. There is no "one thing" that we could have done differently to create the big winning outcome we so badly desired. The reality was a complex decision-tree laden with imperfect information that we navigated well sometimes and badly at others, always under stress and often confronting challenges for the first time. There is a tax for being first-to-market with a new innovation and no or few similar models to learn from, and there is a surcharge on top of this tax when you are a first-time entrepreneur as I was.

Most importantly, reflecting and writing taught me what a gift it was to go through such an intense startup journey from beginning to end, and how the multitude of challenges and failures we — and I — experienced were the source of so much of Zoona's and my growth. As demanding and gut-wrenching as some of these experiences were, I am grateful to have lived through them. "Failure" is something everyone experiences yet few people talk about openly or analyze truthfully, and I have come to believe that embracing failure can offer up a kind of superpower that you need if you want to win, no matter how you define winning.

And so, in reviewing all that we went through, it became apparent to me how many times we had to fail by repeatedly losing battles, until we learned enough and found a way through or around them and on to the next battle. In this framing, the concept of "failing to win" can ultimately be thought of as "failing [in order] to win" — with my penultimate failure serving as the foundation for my new venture.

* * *

This book is organized into three parts.

PART 1, "Founding," walks through my entrepreneurial journey as an idealistic and ambitious young Canadian who was inspired to pursue a purpose-driven career as an entrepreneur in Africa. It concludes with Zoona's $4-million Series A investment round in early 2012 — one of the first on the African continent. In today's digital world where smartphones are ubiquitous, mobile money has transformed payments in Africa, and fintech has become a multi-billion-dollar industry across the globe — with Africa and emerging markets even leading the way. So it's difficult to appreciate just how hard and expensive it was back in 2009 for an unbanked Zambian to send the local equivalent of $20 to another unbanked Zambian to pay for school fees or medicine or something else similarly critical, a problem experienced by millions of people either as senders or receivers. It was equally hard back then for an African startup, let alone one driven by purpose, to raise global venture capital, because the notion of building a huge company that could combine impact with financial returns was largely an unproven concept.

PART 2, "Failing," identifies and analyzes my biggest failures as a first-time CEO of a venture-backed startup responsible for — and ultimately losing — tens of millions of dollars of other people's money, from the Series A through to my unplanned exit. Some failures we recovered from, applying the learnings to achieve new success. Others we did not, or I would still be running the company instead of having written this book. None of these failures was clear to me in the moment — but they are now with the benefit of experience and hindsight.

Finally, **PART 3**, "Winning," explains how the ultimate failure that resulted in my exit from Zoona created new opportunities for future success. These included the motivation for my new startup, Boost, which is built around a set of virtues and principles that were developed to overcome both my formative and Zoona's structural failures.

"Zoona" means "it's real" in the Zambian language of Nyanja, and I have tried my best to tell a real and vulnerable account of my story. I have changed some names to protect privacy, and strived to analyze my failures without personalizing issues or speaking on behalf of others. My goal with sharing this book is to help tilt the odds in favor of all of the courageous entrepreneurs who are trying to make the world a better place for everyone to live in, and not just those like me who come into it with privilege. If this book plays even a small part in doing that, it will be my biggest win of all.

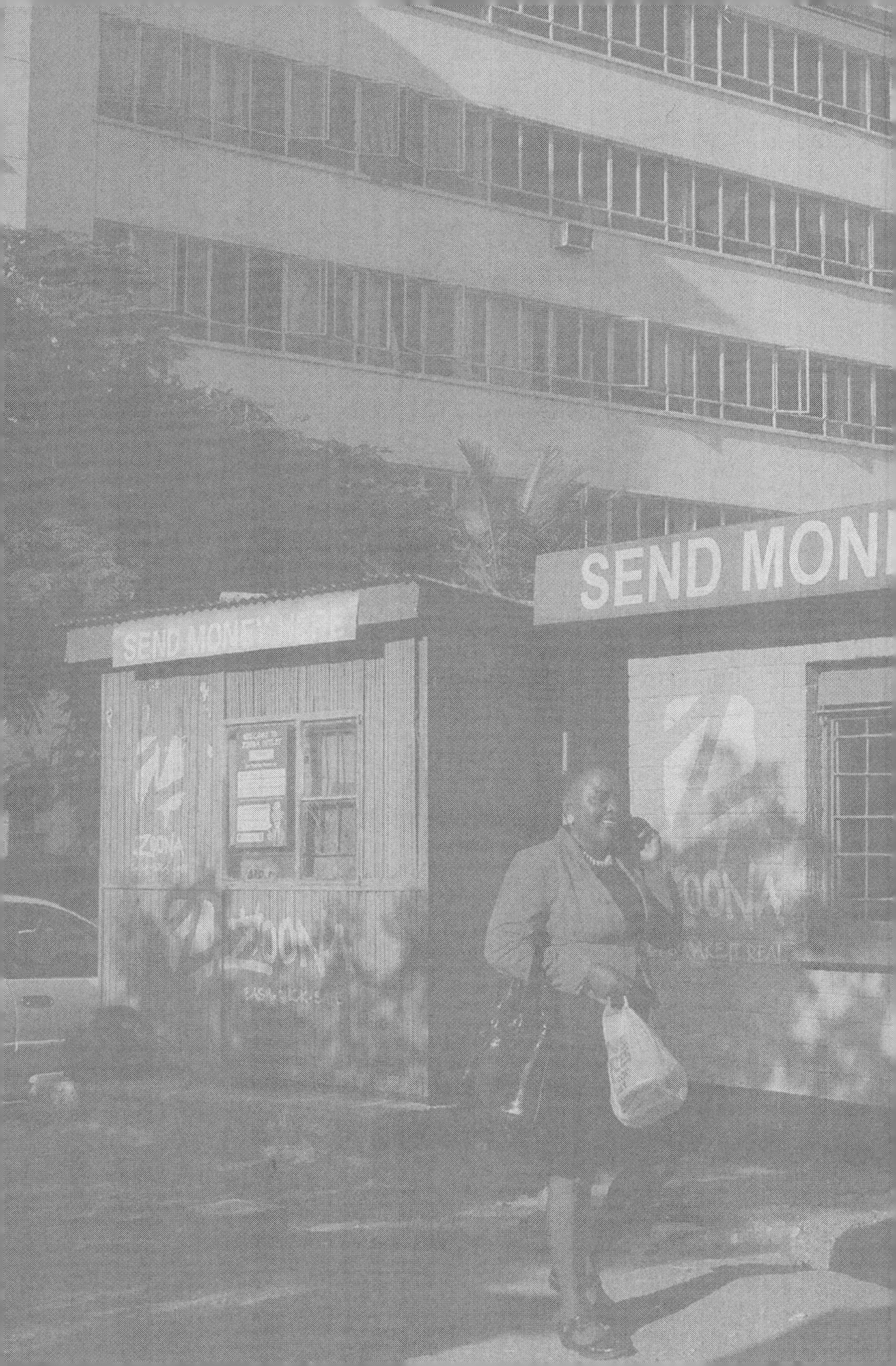
SEND MON
ZOONA

PART 1: FOUNDING

*"Only those who risk going
too far can possibly find out
how far one can go."*
– T.S. ELIOT

CHAPTER 1

ORIGINS

I flew into Lusaka on a Saturday morning in early February 2009. It was a muggy day, typical for the Zambian capital in the rainy season, and as the plane touched down I felt my heart beating faster in my chest. I was excited to be back in a country that had already given me so much.

As a kid growing up in a middle-class home in Calgary, Canada in the 1980s and '90s, Africa had never featured in my life plans. In retrospect, though, the path I have taken was perhaps not an unlikely one. My parents, Don and Susan Quinn, instilled in my sister and me a clear set of social values from a young age. Both were high-school teachers, feminists and respected educational leaders who constantly advocated for change in a conservative political climate. Family dinner conversations often touched on fighting for what you believe in and making the world more equitable — always distinguished from "equal" — for women and other under-represented groups.

I was also taught to work hard and earn my way if I wanted something, an approach that gained me a partial undergraduate scholarship to study mechanical engineering at the University of British Columbia in Vancouver. In my second-to-last year, I stumbled across the newly formed chapter of a startup organization called Engineers Without Borders Canada (EWB) that would change my life. With a mission to inspire young Canadian engineering students to take action to reduce global poverty, EWB provided me the purpose I had been searching for. In 2003, I attended a national conference with more than a hundred like-minded and idealistic engineering students from across the country, all wanting to put their years of education and training to good use. From that moment on, I was hooked. Upon returning, I told my parents that I had no intention of applying for an engineering job; instead, I would settle for nothing less than becoming an EWB volunteer somewhere in Africa.

I knew almost nothing about Africa at the time, other than its stereotypical image as a place of poverty, but my understanding of the continent would change over 10 months from September 2003 as an EWB volunteer in Ghana. I survived off an all-inclusive $300-per-month stipend and did my best to push myself out of my comfort zone by living in an Accra slum, learning the basics of the local language, and making friends with people who only knew hardship yet never seemed to stop smiling. The project I was involved with supported small rural agro-processing enterprises, and while it experienced some early momentum, this ultimately wasn't sustained. I returned to Canada humbled by how stubborn and persistent poverty is, with my eyes opened to the reality that good intentions over a short period are nowhere near enough to achieve lasting impact.

In early 2005 I signed up for a second EWB tour, even more motivated to make a difference, and found myself in southern Zambia with a 150cc Honda motorbike and a mandate to persuade 600 smallholder farmers to shift from their staple maize crop — which was heavily subsidized by the government but poorly suited to the local climate — to the more drought-resistant sorghum. For 18 months, I worked tirelessly to make the project successful, living in villages and rolling up my sleeves, in an effort to build trust, alongside bewildered farmers surviving on one meal a day. But as was the case in Ghana, my project eventually failed, doomed by a traditional NGO approach and a dependency on donor funding. For a long time, I felt the project could have worked had I stuck around to drive it as an independent entrepreneur, but I was anxious to take a step back and reflect on what my purpose really was before stepping up to execute on it.

Despite any lack of lasting impact, my volunteer experience with EWB was all gain for me, earning me a place to study a master's degree in development management at the London School of Economics (LSE), followed by an MBA at the University of Oxford, where I received a Skoll Scholarship for social entrepreneurship. When I had first applied to volunteer in Africa, filled with unbridled passion to change the world for the better, I hadn't imagined how much that decision would end up benefiting *me*. Rather than shy away from this injustice, I embraced it as motivation and set myself the challenge of making my privilege count.

So, when I landed in Lusaka in February 2009, I felt focused and ready to commit.

First Meeting

My pockets were filled with business cards inscribed with a picture of a baobab tree and the words "African Enterprise Partners," a venture I had dreamt up at Oxford with a mission to connect global impact investors with purpose-driven African entrepreneurs building scalable businesses. I had met countless impact investors — at the time they were known as "social investors" — who would talk about how they struggled to find "deal flow" in Africa. There were development projects funded by donors and run by NGOs, and there were commercial businesses funded by cash flow and run by entrepreneurs maximizing profit with little appetite to dilute equity to external investors, especially those who valued social impact on par with financial returns. But there was little or no startup ecosystem, or venture capital, especially in a small landlocked market like Zambia with just 13 million people and a GDP per capita of barely $1,160 per year.

To me, though, this "no deal flow" hypothesis felt false. I knew from experience that Africa was awash with entrepreneurs, many of whom were working tirelessly to solve hard problems for their communities and — with the right capital and support — had the potential to scale. The real problem was that these entrepreneurs didn't know that impact capital from foreign investors even existed, let alone how they might access it.

In 2008, I sent a first draft of a pitch deck for African Enterprise Partners to an Oxford social enterprise lecturer named Kim Alter, a practitioner who brought a refreshingly real-world approach to her classes. She helped me refine it further and then connected me with Agnes Dasewicz, the chief investment officer of the Grassroots Business Fund (GBF), a US-based impact investor. I struck a three-month deal with GBF to source impact investment opportunities in Zambia based on my familiarity with the market, and I committed to sticking around for the long run to help build any company they invested in in return for a small slice of the equity.

I also happened to be in love, and took the opportunity to propose to my girlfriend of 18 months, Isabelle, whom I had met at LSE. Isabelle was a British-Italian development worker, born in Nigeria and raised in French West Africa. Thankfully, she was both keen to move back to Africa and to marry me, so we set off from London together.

Shortly before flying, I sent an email to an American in Lusaka I knew named Mike Field, who worked for a USAID-funded project that involved EWB. Having reviewed my one-page summary of African Enterprise Partners, he put me in touch with two brothers, Brad and Brett Magrath. Brad replied almost immediately with a pitch deck for their startup, Mobile Transactions, and said he would love to meet. I was filled with optimism, having already discovered some of that elusive investor "deal flow."

The Mobile Transactions concept was intriguing. The Magraths planned to enable low-cost payment and transaction services in a cash economy where more than 80 percent of adults didn't have bank accounts and the majority didn't own a mobile phone. Mobile Transactions would use a network of human agents armed with internet-enabled feature phones to power "over-the-counter" consumer money transfers and cash-in and cash-out transactions for corporate (or "enterprise") clients. They had secured a new type of Bank of Zambia license as a "designated payment system" along with $350,000 of equity investment from Dunavant, a large international cotton company that faced the enormous challenge, each harvest season, of paying tens of millions of dollars in cash to 130,000 unbanked and very rural Zambian smallholder farmers.

I met Brad on the Monday morning following my arrival at the Mobile Transactions office in Lusaka's Light Industrial Area — a maze of roads jammed with flatbed trucks and lorries hauling big loads. The office was across the compound from the Zambian headquarters of Dunavant, and was the last place on earth I would have expected to find one of Africa's very first fintech startups.

Brad greeted me enthusiastically and led me past a giant Mobile Transactions banner with a strikingly detailed payment-flow diagram into a square room with desks around the perimeter facing the walls. He then introduced me to Binoy George, who was starting his new role as operations manager that same day. There were a number of young Zambian men buzzing about the office. "Barclays Bank just let go of a bunch of their commissioned sales staff because of the global financial crisis," Brad told me with some jubilation, "so we are scooping them up for our launch!"

We walked across the compound to the Dunavant building and upstairs to a boardroom, where I hooked my laptop up to a projector as Brad's younger brother Brett arrived. Brad introduced Brett as the "brains" behind the Mobile Transactions payment system — as well as the flow diagram on their branded banner — and also the managing director of their technology company in Cape Town. Brett had been pulled out of a meeting with Dunavant to see my presentation, and he didn't seem as keen to meet me as his brother had been.

I explained my goals while flipping through a few slides on African Enterprise Partners and the Grassroots Business Fund. Brad then took me through the Mobile Transactions deck, confidently proclaiming that they were going to digitize payments across Zambia's entire agriculture sector before expanding across Africa with corporate partners like Dunavant. The plan was to be cash-flow positive in six months and to partner with a strategic bank; they were already in investment discussions with a South African bank with a pan-African footprint. Brett filled in the details of how their payment system worked and how they had designed, built and implemented a system for Dunavant to track and reconcile payments to their smallholder cotton farmers.

My first meeting could not have gone any better. "These guys have the potential to transform Africa!" I exclaimed over lunch with Isabelle. "I don't think I'm going to find a better opportunity."

"Well, that was easy," she said, observing how I had accomplished my three-month goal by lunchtime on day one.

I set up a call with Agnes and her team at GBF. She was optimistic, but didn't quite believe that I had found the best investment opportunity in the country — and maybe on the continent! — in my first meeting on my first day. Nonetheless, she gave me the green light to do more research on Mobile Transactions while urging me to continue scouting.

Brad and Brett

I spent a few more weeks in Zambia and met with several other companies until I had to leave the country because of a quirky immigration rule while my work permit was pending. This gave me the opportunity to fly with Isabelle to Cape Town and meet up with Brett to learn more about his technology company. He had warmed up to me since our first meeting, and offered to pick us up at the airport and let us stay at his house.

The next morning Brett drove us to his office, located in a business park in a suburb of Cape Town called Brooklyn. I had imagined a buzzing office of software developers, a vision of a Silicon Valley startup in my head. Instead, Brett led me into an office barely twice the size of the one in Zambia with a lone desk in the middle of the barren room. There were stairs leading up to a loft with two more empty desks for the company's developers, Konrad and Aubrey — "when they are here," as Brett explained. Aubrey had a second job while Konrad sometimes worked from "home," which at the time was an extension of Brett's house.

I was unnerved by the empty office, but then Brett scribbled out diagrams of the Mobile Transactions payment system, complete with several products he had come up with and built from scratch. I learned that like me, Brett was an extreme extrovert and seemed to relish having someone to talk to in person. We resonated with each other's enthusiasm, and by the end of the day it felt as if we had known each other for years.

One night over dinner Brett told me the origin story of Mobile Transactions.

Brad and Brett were both second-generation Zambians born in Kitwe, Zambia's second-largest city in the economic heartland, the central Copperbelt Province. When Brett was a toddler and Brad was nine, their parents divorced and their mother moved to Singapore with her new husband. As they grew up, they divided their time between the two countries, as well as South Africa, where they attended boarding school.

After finishing university in South Africa, Brad took a corporate job as the general manager of a South African paint company and grew the Zambian unit into its top-performing subsidiary. He then worked for Telecel, Africa's first mobile phone company, where he came to realize that he was sick of working in corporate jobs and was longing to break out on his own as an entrepreneur.

Meanwhile, Brett had moved to London to work as a business analyst for J.P. Morgan. During a performance appraisal one day, he was told he was on track to take over his boss's job in the future if he kept up his good performance. This unappealing prospect was the push he needed to quit immediately and take the plunge to start a business with his brother.

The two felt there was great opportunity in Africa's mobile phone industry, which was growing exponentially. Brett hired Konrad and Aubrey to build an airtime distribution system that would calculate and pay multi-tiered commissions, from a mobile network operator (MNO) at the top all the way down to a sole trader on the street who sold airtime (pre-paid mobile phone credit) scratch cards for less than a dollar. They signed a partnership contract with a Malawian MNO and hired Binoy as their general manager.

Over two years, they built the Malawi business to the point that it was processing $2-million a month in airtime sales, but it proved difficult to translate this top-line growth into positive cash flow, so they decided to shut it down and monetize what they could to start their next venture. They flew to Malawi together to tell Binoy, who showed up the next day with a man who wanted to buy the business — and had a car trunk full of Malawian kwacha to make it happen. They accepted the cash and had a fun time trying to convert it into a currency they could use outside of Malawi.

A few months later, Brad went out for beers in Lusaka with his friend Mike Field, the man who would eventually introduce me to the Magraths. Mike shared with him some of the problems in Zambia's cotton sector; for instance, how companies like Dunavant had to transport truckloads of cash down bumpy dirt roads through rural villages with security guards armed with AK-47s. And how farmers had to line up to receive cash for their cotton at designated pay points, placing inked thumbprints to prove receipt on paper documents that later had to be reconciled. It was a high-risk and inefficient system, with no alternatives.

The next morning, Brad passed this problem on to Brett, who started thinking about how he could apply their previous learnings from Malawi and build a new transaction system to solve at least part of this problem. He designed a system that would validate and reconcile all farmer payments in real time, captured by a field agent with a netbook computer connected to the internet over a GPRS cellular network. The data would beam to a centralized server that management could access from anywhere in the world. The farmer would still be paid in cash, but with dramatically improved controls and real-time data for Dunavant.

The brothers secured a commitment of $200,000 in grant funding to start this project from the USAID project PROFIT, where Mike worked. They used this to build the system and kicked off a pilot project in the rural town of Katete, located four hours east of Lusaka in the nation's cotton heartland. During the first batch of 580 successful payment transactions, one of the Zambian farmers conveyed his surprise and delight in his local language, Nyanja. *"Ni zoona!"*, he exclaimed — "It's real!" Brad and Brett decided to brand the product "Zoona" (pronounced zo-oh-na).

Dunavant was excited enough by the pilot to invite the brothers to present to the company's senior management in Geneva. Brett flew to Switzerland and led the pitch, with Brad dialing in. The Dunavant team immediately offered to invest $350,000 in the business in exchange for a 35 percent equity stake. They also suggested changing the name from "Zoona" to something more corporate-friendly, and Mobile Transactions was born.

Inspired by M-Pesa

Around the same time, a tech innovation in Kenya was starting to make waves. It was called M-Pesa, and it was led by Safaricom, Kenya's largest MNO. Safaricom consumers could register for M-Pesa mobile wallets and use their mobile phones to send a person-to-person (P2P) money transfer to any other M-Pesa wallet for a low fee. They could also make deposits into or withdraw cash from their wallets at registered M-Pesa agents. Any retail shop with a mobile phone and cash float could sign up as an agent and earn commission on every cash-in or cash-out transaction. With M-Pesa, Safaricom had essentially created a low-cost and widely distributed human ATM network that enabled all of their consumers to store money, send and receive money transfers, buy airtime and pay their bills using even the most basic mobile phone, without any need for a bank account. This was an extraordinary innovation at the time, even by global standards, and Brad and Brett were taking note.

While the opportunity in the Zambian cotton sector was large, it was also seasonal. Eager to generate a more sustainable cash flow, and wanting to retain some independence from Dunavant, the brothers had been wondering if a service similar to M-Pesa could work in Zambia, where the only formal way people could send and receive money was through a parastatal post office network, which had a limited distribution footprint and charged the exorbitantly high minimum fee of 12 percent for a money transfer. Unlike Safaricom, however, the brothers didn't have a brand, consumer base or distribution network. They also couldn't develop a mobile wallet on a SIM card because they weren't an MNO, they didn't have the capital to become one, and the Zambian MNOs would never grant them access to their SIM cards.

So, Brett reconfigured their farmer payment system to register agents and pay them real-time commissions for cash-in and cash-out transactions. They then designed a product where unregistered consumers could send and receive "over-the-counter" (OTC, as it became known) money transfers processed by agents. The money transfer sender (who had the cash) would pay a fee, while the receiver (who needed the cash) wouldn't. This was contrary to the M-Pesa economics, which were driven by cash-out charges. M-Pesa also provided users with mobile wallets to store value, but this was not a market need in Zambia at time. Even the vast majority of M-Pesa P2P transactions in Kenya were cashed out by receivers immediately.

I listened in awe as Brett told this story from start to finish. It seemed like a perfect fit for GBF's mission and a great first deal for African Enterprise Partners. The brothers had the entrepreneurial track record, technology, regulatory license, strategic partner, market opportunity and vision. More than that, I felt they shared my values, and were genuinely good human beings. Even though I hadn't explored any other opportunities in detail in Zambia, I found myself desperately wanting to work with them.

I updated GBF and persuaded them to enter into formal due diligence after presenting to their investment committee over a voice call. It went well, short of one awkward discussion about the fact that Brad and Brett were white Africans, which did not exactly offer GBF the front-of-website image of social entrepreneurs it was seeking. To be honest, they didn't fit the profile I was envisioning either when dreaming up African Enterprise Partners, but there was no doubt that Brad and Brett were purpose-driven African entrepreneurs building a potentially scalable business that could make a huge impact if successful.

Fortunately, the GBF investment committee voted to proceed. After a brief due diligence, the $200,000 investment closed on July 1, 2009. GBF structured it as convertible debt with a revenue share "kicker," meaning that GBF would have an option to convert their investment into equity at a discount if we could raise future equity; otherwise they would get a share of company revenue until they earned a capped return. GBF also committed to paying me a monthly retainer for a year for 50 percent of my salary from a technical assistance grant they had allocated alongside their investment. For the other 50 percent, Brad and Brett agreed to give me an equivalent amount of sweat equity in Mobile Transactions, which we sealed with a simple MOU and handshake.

The First Money Transfer

After returning to Lusaka with a work permit and approval for GBF to commence due diligence, I officially set up a desk in the Mobile Transactions office. My timing couldn't have been better, as it coincided with the signing up of our very first agents. Armed with an agent contract that Brett had adapted from the internet, Brad sent out his team of sales generators across the country. Each sales generator was responsible for identifying retail shops that had steady foot traffic, and then convincing the owner to sign the contract. The agent would then have to deposit the Zambian kwacha equivalent of $500 into our client bank account in order to be credited with a matching value of electronic float — no small ask for a small business owner, especially as we were an unknown company with no consumers. The agent also received a Nokia 3120 mobile phone with a pre-loaded Opera Mini web browser (which could be opened via a GPRS or Edge data connection), two posters, a signboard and a metal wall mount featuring the call to action, "Transact Here," along with our logo. The logo consisted of a green, red and yellow ball that Brett had designed to symbolize agricultural, corporate and money transfer payments, respectively, with three arrows depicting their interconnectivity

After several agents miraculously signed up and made their initial deposits in exchange for their electronic floats, we were naively expecting a pent-up flood of consumer demand that replicated the exponential growth of M-Pesa in Kenya, which we had read about with great interest. Unlike M-Pesa, however, we weren't backed by an MNO with a household brand, huge distribution network and millions of loyal consumers, so in hindsight it's not surprising that things didn't quite work out this way. But the first ever money transfer, sent on April Fools' Day, 2009, was thrilling nonetheless.

The sending customer showed up at our only agent in the town of Nakonde, population 10,000, on the Zambia-Tanzania border. The $200 he wanted to send was far larger than the $30 average transaction size we had anticipated based on studying M-Pesa. Our sales generator in Nakonde, Claudius Fundi, called Binoy from the agent's shop, and he in turn called Brett on Skype. Together, they validated that the sending agent had enough electronic float in his Mobile Transactions account (or else the transaction would have failed), and Claudius walked the customer and agent through the sending flow while we all held our breath.

There was a collective exhale when we saw the confirmation message on our system and the customer received an SMS saying the same. But the relief was short-lived once we remembered that the receiver might not be able to find an agent, or that the agent might not have the cash to pay out. Claudius spoke to the sender, who told him the transfer was going to Mazabuka, another small town, this one south of Lusaka, population 35,000. When Binoy called our recently registered agent there, the receiving customer was already in his shop showing him the SMS that said he had been sent a Mobile Transactions money transfer. Binoy validated that the agent had enough cash and walked him through the transaction on the phone. Once our system showed us a second confirmation message, we checked back with Claudius in Nakonde, who confirmed that the sender had also received a second SMS stating his money transfer had been collected. Binoy called both agents, who confirmed that they could see their commissions in their electronic accounts. The entire sequence had taken about 20 minutes.

This may not seem impressive by today's digital standards, but at the time it was groundbreaking. Claudius asked the sending customer how he normally sent money to Mazabuka, which he would do on a monthly basis to support a dependent. Before Mobile Transactions, he'd had two options. He would find a bus or lorry driver heading to Mazabuka and negotiate a fee, typically 10 to 20 percent, to carry the cash — with the distinct possibility that the driver would steal the lot. Alternatively, he would *make the 17-hour car journey himself.* Unsurprisingly, the customer was ecstatic with his first Mobile Transactions experience and he told Claudius he would use our service every time from now on. Nothing like this had existed in Zambia before — or Africa, for that matter, outside of Kenya.

Citizen's Arrest

With this milestone achieved, we turned our attention to our home base in Lusaka. Unfortunately, the sales generator had managed to sign up just a solitary agent, the owner of an internet cafe along Cairo Road, the busy high street in the center of the city. I went to see this cafe for myself, walking half an hour from our office, which was preferable to sitting in traffic. I searched up and down the street for it, with no luck. After calling our sales generator for directions, I finally found the building and walked up two flights of dimly lit stairs to the entrance around the back. Sure enough, there was a Mobile Transactions wall mount, poster and A-frame signboard on display. I greeted the owner, who told me he had yet to deposit funds into our client bank account. In other words, all of our branding was on display but the agent was unable to transact. Luckily for us, no consumers had come asking.

Not far away, at the midpoint of Cairo Road, stood Lusaka's central post office. For several days after payday, dozens of people could be seen standing in long queues to send money to family dependents, setting them back at least 12 percent in fees in the process. Besides the high cost, the post office was closed by 3 p.m. on weekdays and didn't open on weekends, the working hours of a parastatal entity in an uncompetitive market. We also learned that many rural post offices could go for weeks without cash, which meant that receivers would have to come back several times before collecting their money. All this hassle multiplied the total transaction cost to the customer.

I called Brad, who walked over to meet me on Cairo Road. After visiting our invisible and illiquid agent, we walked down the street to the main post office. It was mid-afternoon in early April 2009; the queues were enormous and closing time was approaching. Brad had brought a stack of Mobile Transactions flyers and we started handing them out to people, attracting an eager audience. We explained that our new money transfer service was significantly cheaper, but withheld the part that we didn't yet have an agent nearby who could actually serve any consumers.

Suddenly, a tall, angry-looking man in a suit pushed through the crowd. "You are soliciting my customers!" he shouted. "I am putting you under citizen's arrest!" His name tag identified him as the "Postmaster." Brad immediately went into battle mode, puffing out his chest and responding forcefully. "Zambia is a free market and we are allowed to be here!" he declared. While they argued loudly, I stood to the side and then edged toward the exit. After the postmaster repeated his threat of putting us under citizen's arrest, Brad followed him up to his fourth-floor office while I sheepishly made my escape.

I went outside and waited anxiously for Brad at a small island in the parking lot barely 20 feet from the post office entrance, which everyone going in and out had to pass by. Ten minutes later, he emerged with his trademark ear-to-ear grin and told me he had reached an agreement with the postmaster. We could freely solicit customers as long as we stayed off post office property. That meant the little island we were standing on was fair game.

The First Champion Agent

We savored our first competitive victory, and continued handing out flyers and chatting with people walking to and from the post office entrance. "We need an agent right here," I said. "This would be the perfect location to target the post office foot traffic."

Brad and I looked at each other and then at a small standalone shop behind us, where two young men were playing checkers and selling airtime scratch cards to passers-by. We approached and learned that one of them had an aunt who rented the building from the Lusaka city council. Brad asked for her number and then called her, offering a guaranteed monthly rental fee equivalent to what she made from the profits of her shop. After a quick conversation, she agreed. We had our flagship location.

The following Monday, we showed up with a painter, a small

army of sales generators and a box full of cash. We took over the shop and painted it with the Mobile Transactions brand and logo, then stopped people on their way to the post office to tell them about our new money transfer service. A few early adopters tried us out, offering valuable information about their transaction behavior and feedback on our pricing. We also learned where the money transfers were being sent, which prompted Brad to send sales generators to set up agents in the prominent pay-out locations. He also directed Binoy to send the sales generators their per diems for accommodation and return travel by money transfer, so that the only way they could redeem them was if they set up a Mobile Transactions agent who actually had cash.

Our daily transaction numbers started to climb. We celebrated as we hit 10 sends per day. Our Cairo Road outlet became a sending hub while our sales generators activated new agents in pay-out locations across the country. Binoy shouted out loud every time we completed a transaction.

Our transaction numbers grew each day, but then plateaued at around 30. As part of our investigation as to why, we audited our Cairo Road shop and discovered missing cash. Some of our sales generators had found an easier way to make money than working: They just put the cash in their pockets. This was the first of many problems to come with commissioned field staff being tempted by cash, combined with our loose or non-existent controls. At that stage, we were more concerned with gaining traction and figured we could plug the holes as we found them.

We had no real desire to manage the shop ourselves, so we decided to make one of our (seemingly honest) sales generators a micro-franchisee. The Cairo Road shop would be his to manage and he would earn commissions on every transaction. We would invest the float, pay the rent and retain the right to fire and replace him if he broke any serious rule or customer service standard. We called him a "champion agent" to differentiate from all of our other "retail agents," which were typical in the M-Pesa model.

For the sales generator, this was an amazing proposition. With no cash at risk (as he had none to risk), he could be his own boss and earn 20 percent of the fee on every sending and receiving money transfer. We also guaranteed him a minimum base income to cover his downside for a period (and reduce the risk that he would run away with the cash). If he worked hard, there was no limit on his upside. If he didn't or stole the money, he would risk giving up a recurring and growing income stream, and join Zambia's swathes of unemployed youth.

We could afford to take the risk on the float because the margins on a money transfer were good, even though our average fee of 7 percent of the money transfer value was much lower than what the post office charged. We shared 40 percent of this with the sending and receiving agents, and kept the remaining 60 percent — which meant that if we invested $500 of float at our risk to kickstart a champion agent, we could expect to break even after 400 average transfers of $30. We knew by the queues at the post office next door that the demand existed to achieve this volume many times over.

The next day, our first champion agent showed up for work dressed proudly in a tie at 8 a.m. — an hour earlier than his arrival time when he was a mere sales generator. The Mobile Transactions flag, which had been slumped in front of the Cairo Road shop the previous week, stood erect. He worked noticeably harder all morning, almost dragging new customers into his shop, and he broke the previous daily transaction record by 1 p.m.

Doubling Down

We knew we were onto something, so we took another sales generator and made him a champion agent right next to another busy Lusaka post office — with the same positive effect. Money transfer sends started growing again, though it was hardly plain sailing. We were now having constant problems at the other end of the transaction, paying out cash to receivers, especially in the populous Copperbelt Province.

I decided to look into it personally, and made the six-hour drive north with one of our first and most trustworthy sales generators, Teddy Sampa. We started with the city of Ndola, the region's industrial center and Zambia's third-largest city. We tracked down several customers who had been sent money but were yet to receive it. Binoy had registered me as an agent in our system so that I could find these customers and personally pay out their money transfers, along with an apology for the hassle and delay. We then drove 45 minutes up the road to Kitwe, Brad and Brett's hometown.

After spending several frustrating days trying to track down our elusive agents, who had all been set up by our one and only Copperbelt sales generator, I felt like I was back on Cairo Road right at the start looking for something that wasn't there. When I finally found an agent, he irately explained how he had deposited money into our client bank account but never received a corresponding electronic credit on our system. After an investigation, I realized that our sales generator had given the agent his own bank account and stolen the money. Teddy called around and managed to track him down at the local Barclays Bank, where he had somehow gotten his old job back without telling us. We showed up at the Barclays sales office unannounced, and I spotted him running away after he caught sight of us at the entrance. I stormed past reception and found him hiding in a broom closet in the back corner of the open-plan office, where I formally fired him in front of all his Barclays colleagues and threatened to come back with the police if the money wasn't refunded to the defrauded agent by the end of the day. Lucky for him, he still had it and gave it all back.

Unfortunately, with our lack of controls and ineffective operational management, we played this game of cat and mouse with crooked sales generators and poor agents again and again. It became a regular part of my job to drive from town to town only to find that our sales generators or agents were stealing money. Our two Lusaka champion agents were becoming money transfer-sending engines, but this wouldn't matter if the receivers had negative experiences every time they tried to collect their cash.

To overcome this challenge, we decided to double down on the champion-agent model and roll it out in key cities and towns across the country. To bolster our on-the-ground support, I reached out to Engineers Without Borders for help, and they offered to send us a Canadian volunteer named Graham Lettner at no cost for at least a year.

With Graham on board, Teddy drove the two of us back up to the Copperbelt. Our first priority was to set up a champion agent in Kitwe. Like Lusaka, Kitwe had a main post office right in the center of town that developed long queues of money transfer consumers after pay day. There were no standalone shops that we could take over, but there was a small shopping mall right across the street from the post office with a number of empty stores. We tracked down the landlord of one of them and negotiated the rent, which we paid in cash.

Now we needed a champion agent. Teddy made a phone call and introduced us to a 22-year-old woman named Sandra

Jere. She was shy and had no previous experience running a cash business or serving customers, but Teddy assured us she would show up for work and wouldn't steal the money — our only real standards at the time. I gave her a hastily drafted champion agent contract — which I had adapted from Brett's adapted agent contract — to sign, and Teddy set her up with an account on our system. While Teddy trained her how to process transactions, I called Binoy and asked him to issue her with our standard $500 float. We had run out of agent branding materials, so Teddy told Sandra to make a signboard by hand and start transacting right away. We told her that *if* she did well on her own, *then* we would come back to brand her shop. And that was the extent of our champion agent onboarding.

We got in our truck for the long drive back to Lusaka. "Is it right, what we just did?" Graham asked me as we pulled out of Kitwe. "I mean, we just found a young woman, told her to sign a piece of paper that she didn't read, and basically said, 'Good luck, you're on your own!' before driving away." It was a good question.

We replicated this pattern over the following weeks and months, with gradual improvements, setting up champion agents next to post offices across the country. It was hard work, but we somehow managed to establish reliable sending and receiving corridors in all the key cities and towns, as well as several rural areas that surprised us. Transactions started to grow steadily month-on-month without us spending any money on consumer advertising. Demand was entirely driven by word of mouth, and most new consumers we acquired would use us again the following month, becoming familiar to their local agents.

Champion agents also started emerging on their own, some from right under our noses. During one of the several cash-flow crises we navigated after burning through GBF's investment, we were unable to renew a contract for a 22-year-old data-entry clerk named Misozi Mkandiwire, who faced the significant challenge of finding another job with only a high-school diploma in an economy rife with youth unemployment. She had $500 to her name, and upon leaving asked if we could make her a champion agent at an outlet she had scouted further down Cairo Road. We agreed, but because of our own cash-flow situation we could not lend her any more money for float, so she gambled with her own $500. To her surprise and delight, she more than doubled her money in her first month. This really opened her eyes, so she made a big effort to get to know all of her customers, who in turn kept coming back to send money each month. After noticing a contrasting downward slide in performance of our original Cairo Road champion agent, we terminated his contract and offered Misozi the chance to take over. She jumped at the opportunity, hired some of her family members to help her as tellers, and soon found herself managing two of our flagship champion agent outlets.

In the coming years, Misozi would expand her operation to 26 outlets in Lusaka, employing 43 young tellers and processing over $1-million per month in transactions. She would eventually leave her business to some of her family members and tellers to take up a new challenge as our Zambian managing director. Meanwhile in Kitwe, the seemingly shy Sandra would expand her champion agent business to 16 outlets, employing 23 tellers. By the age of 28, her father would be working for her to help move cash around, and she would have built a house from scratch out of her profits. This is what our company was about: Perfectly combining purpose with profit.

But this is getting ahead of the story. The path to success was fraught with obstacles, and the biggest of all was invariably cash flow.

CHAPTER 2

A CASHLESS AFRICA

"Why do we exist and what's our inspirational dream?"

I wrote this on the whiteboard with Brad and Brett watching, arms behind their heads as they reclined in their chairs. It was August 2009, and our first ever meeting to come up with a vision, mission and long-term strategy. I was nervous, wondering if these two seasoned and older entrepreneur brothers would have the patience for my business-school speak.

Brad's hand shot up as if he were back at school. "Breakfast with Bill!" he shouted — as in Bill Gates. We laughed, but Brad was serious. He was always great at easing awkward situations.

I probed deeper.

"What is the inspiration that's going to drive us every day so that we can change the world and one day actually have breakfast with Bill?"

There was silence, then Brad's hand shot up again.

"A cashless Africa," he said.

We sat in silence for a few more moments. *A cashless Africa*. It captured the level of our ambition and was surely an inspirational dream. It also reflected our vision of a digital future. Even though we had launched as a cash-based money transfer service, Brett had always insisted that this was just a stepping stone. He was already designing several new products that were years ahead of their time.

The Unlikely Angel

Without more cash in the bank, our dream would be short-lived. Our Grassroots Business Fund investment was rapidly dwindling, so I reached out to the only angel investor I knew — who also happened to be the CFO of Google.

I first met Patrick Pichette at the 2003 Engineers Without Borders national conference that had set me on my journey to Africa. Patrick was EWB's board chair and one of the organization's first angel investors. A few years later, at another EWB conference, I had a chance to attend a workshop where he shared his personal story, from growing up in a traditional francophone household in Quebec to becoming a partner at McKinsey & Company and then an executive at Canada's largest telco. I'll never forget his closing advice: "Take one big step plus one little step outside of your comfort zone, and stay there. Any further out you are at risk of crashing and burning, but any closer you are not pushing yourself enough."

In 2008, Patrick became the CFO of Google, a remarkable achievement for an "insecure overachiever," as he liked to call himself. Patrick knew who I was thanks to a blog I wrote during my EWB placements, and one post in particular which was read by the singer Sarah McLachlan and inspired her music video *World On Fire*, raising funding for EWB and gaining me some notoriety in the process. I brazenly tracked down his personal email address from a contact at EWB, mailed him a few times to tell him what I was up to and then sent him a pitch deck for Mobile Transactions, letting him know we'd love to have him as an angel investor. To my surprise and delight, he replied.

> I shared your business plan with a few VCs/angel investors here [at Google]. Here is the summary of their comments:
>
> "If I were to decide for me, I would likely not invest in this venture... There is team, technology, business model and execution risk, along with Africa risk layered on top."
>
> Having said this, I am still interested to see what's missing in making this work. We should carve out at least 60 minutes to discuss.

I completely overlooked the critique from his colleagues, and was simply thrilled Patrick had replied without saying "no!" I was expecting a polite decline — instead, I had 60 minutes to convince the CFO of Google that we were the most exciting early-stage investment opportunity in Africa.

One phone call turned into several more, with Patrick asking me questions about the business and coaching me on which metrics to track. He then offered to have a call with Brad and Brett. I'm not sure they had believed me when I first told them that the CFO of Google was taking an interest in investing in us — they had been rather nonchalant about it, perhaps understandably. But that phone call convinced them. Patrick started with some honest and critical feedback, telling us we were on the right track and that we had a huge opportunity in front of us. Presciently, he warned us that if we didn't move fast, the big mobile network operators (MNOs) would take over and destroy us. Then he offered to invest and become our board chair.

It was a surreal offer. We were stunned, then elated — before being yanked back to earth.

Given Patrick's position at Google, his personal investments needed prior approval from Google's governance committee. Several weeks passed, and then he called me to share the disappointing news that Google had concerns and had precluded him from directly investing in our company. I was devastated; he also appeared genuinely upset by the setback.

He apologized, but then proposed an alternative. As long as he remained at arm's length from Mobile Transactions, he could lend *me* a smaller amount, while also becoming my personal mentor. I drafted a simple MOU between us, and within a couple of days he had wired the cash into my Canadian bank account. As soon as I could, I forwarded the money to our nearly depleted Mobile Transactions bank account — and with that, the company gained a cash-flow boost and I gained a seasoned executive as a mentor.

Chicken or Pig?

But we still needed more money.

I flew to Cape Town to meet with Brett as the 2010 Football World Cup was playing out in stadiums across South Africa — a first for the continent, opening many international eyes to the potential of Africa. We could quite literally feel the electricity of it all, because our new (and smaller) office was on the fan walk from the train station to the brand-new football stadium. As the drumbeats and vuvuzelas sounded in the background, we went through our accounts and gained a shared understanding of our financial reality. We reached two conclusions. First, we needed a CFO to take ownership of our financial accounts and cash flow, which were in a mess. Second, we had nearly burned through all of our GBF investment and had two months to go before we ran out of cash.

What followed was an honest conversation about whether

I truly wanted to be a partner and co-founder with Brad and Brett. "When you have bacon and eggs for breakfast, the chicken is involved but the pig is committed," they told me. "Which one are you, Mike?"

If I chose to be a "pig," they would carve out more equity for me, provided I could come up with $100,000 to invest. I didn't have the money, but I did want a bigger equity stake. I promised to figure something out, which soon led to a pair of crucial decisions that would make my stake a very personal one indeed.

I knew that, before anything else, we needed to solve the financial management issue, so I flew to Johannesburg with Isabelle to visit Keith Davies, a friend from my Oxford MBA class. We all met for dinner on the patio of a buzzing restaurant in Sandton outside the South African head office of Citibank, where he worked. Almost as soon as we arrived, Keith launched into a long rant about how badly he wanted a fresh start. He told us about his idea to quit his job to start an advisory business helping small companies in Africa with financial management and discipline.

My adrenalin was pumping. I knew Keith was the guy we needed. He was trustworthy and experienced, and everyone who knew him respected him highly and vouched for his bedrock integrity. So, without naming my other partners, I told him about the Mobile Transactions vision of creating a cashless Africa, concluding with an offer in the form of a plea: "We are desperate for a CFO and a fourth partner. Will you join us?"

The next day, I took Keith through our pitch deck, and when I mentioned the name Brett Magrath he stopped me. "Hold on," he said. "Do you mean Toad Magrath?"

I couldn't believe the coincidence — "Toad" was a nickname Brett's wife and friends frequently used. Keith told me the two of them had been students at the prestigious Hilton boarding school at the same time. Brett was his senior, and as part of boarding-school hierarchy Keith had to spend his first year worshiping at Brett's feet whenever he walked by.

Thankfully, Keith had moved past those indignities of tradition and was keen to join us. I arranged for him to meet with Brad at Johannesburg's OR Tambo International Airport, and he gave his approval. Brett vaguely remembered Keith from boarding school and didn't feel the need for a meeting; if Brad and I were both happy bringing him on board, he was too. Keith promptly gave his notice at the bank and began making plans to close down his life in Johannesburg and prepare to take on his new role as quickly as possible.

While the CFO problem was solved, we were still running out of cash, a fact I had omitted in my sales pitch to Keith. I had to solve the second problem: Coming up with $100,000.

I had no idea how. At the time I wasn't even drawing a salary, only sweat equity, while Isabelle and I lived off her income as technical director of evaluation at World Vision, a global NGO. The sweat equity demonstrated my commitment to the company, but it had no bearing on my pledge to put cash on the table. On top of it all, I had a mountain of student debt that I had stopped paying down when my GBF income ended.

I started researching whether it was possible to get a personal bank loan. I had bank accounts in the U.K. and Canada, but I was ineligible to borrow from either of them while living in Africa, and I couldn't borrow from a Zambian bank on my non-resident work permit. Given my financial history, I doubt any bank would have thought me creditworthy anyway.

I started contemplating asking my parents for money, but I was reluctant to do so. I didn't want to put them in a vulnerable position and I knew they didn't have $100,000 in the bank. As retired high-school teachers from the Calgary public school system, neither had grown rich and I had never seen them make a risky investment. Most recently, they had used their savings to build a retirement house on Vancouver Island that took them several years to finish.

In August 2010, Isabelle and I flew to Canada for a two-week stay with my family. Every day we were with them I thought about asking my parents for their help, but I couldn't summon the courage. They had always had my back, but I had never needed this kind of support. The two weeks passed, and we flew back to Lusaka.

It wasn't long before I found myself staring at our dire cash-flow projections one evening and realized it was now or never. I typed an email to my mom and dad, outlining my ask and my promise to repay them with interest. I awoke the next morning to my mom's reply: "Every piece of conventional wisdom advises us not to mix money and family, but we love you and believe in you and we are here if you need our help."

The next day they drove to their bank, took out a mortgage on their house and wired the funds directly into the Mobile Transactions bank account. I added this to my MOU with Brad and Brett, and decided to throw in the towel on my personal venture by formally shutting down African Enterprise Partners to become a "pig" in Mobile Transactions. We shook hands again and got back to work — this time as partners.

Going All In

With a minimum $30,000 monthly cash burn, I knew my investment wouldn't last long. I was getting used to running out of cash, and my optimistic nature combined with my volunteering background enabled my belief that we would always find a solution. At the same time, I knew Brad and

Brett thrived under pressure and had plenty of entrepreneurial experience operating on the edge. But for Keith — a recovering investment banker who, unlike the rest of us, was also a prudent saver — running out of cash was a new experience.

In Keith's first month in October 2010, he took over the financial accounts from Brett and set up a new cash-flow forecast. He called me from Cape Town to explain that things were way worse than we thought: "We are eight weeks from being broke!" In addition, he explained, the assumptions we had made to support our revenue projections were too optimistic, and the way we were loosely extending float to our champion agents was draining our cash. Keith asked if he should already start to make plans to take on consulting work, fearing he had joined a company that was dead in the water.

I flew from Lusaka to meet him, and spent the night on his couch. Brett picked us up the next morning, and on the way to our office, Keith laid out the problem from the backseat. While stopped at a red light, Brett clapped his hands and let out a loud belly laugh. "Today is going to be a great day!" he said.

I watched Keith's face contort with confusion. He had just left a cushy job with a global bank to join a startup on the verge of collapsing — and one of his partners was *laughing*?

Brett carried on. "We are always running out of cash, but this time we have revenue and visibility!"

Brett was right: With revenue we had levers to pull and, thanks to Keith, more notice than ever before. We locked ourselves in a room and analyzed every source and use of cash we had. We reworked our money transfer pricing tiers, identified bespoke system-development projects we could take on that would generate upfront payments, made a list of our own payments we could defer, and switched various fixed costs to variable ones. This would extend our runway to make it through to the end of

January, aided by the demand spike in money transfers that we knew would take place between Christmas and the New Year. In addition, there was relief on the horizon: We were working on a major enterprise payment contract with the World Food Programme to facilitate payments to small retailers for food basket subsidies they were issuing to HIV/AIDS beneficiaries. We anticipated that this would kick in by February and break our cycle of running out of cash.

I could tell that Keith wasn't entirely convinced we were going to survive, but he was amazed by our ability to act so quickly. In his previous job, he had been trapped in a corporate bureaucracy without the power to make decisions. Now he was experiencing the adrenalin rush of diagnosing a problem and coming up with a host of potential solutions within a single day.

Despite Keith's obvious anxiety, Brett and I took the opportunity to ask him over lunch if he could come up with some cash to invest in the company. We justified it to him as his chance to become a founding partner, like me, with real skin in the game. I asked him about his personal financial position, and he told us he had $30,000 squirreled away in a pension. Brett and I looked at him and, echoing each other, asked, "Why do you need a pension when you're only 32?"

The next day, Keith took the plunge and liquidated the pension. He also managed to borrow another $15,000 from a mutual Oxford MBA colleague to increase his equity stake and provide us with an additional buffer. We flew to Zambia together, with the cash in Keith's laptop bag. The next morning Keith drove to the bank and made a deposit into our company bank account. He then drove back to our Lusaka office, logged into our online bank account and watched the balance plummet as he paid staff salaries and outstanding invoices. As with my investment, this was all done on a handshake and simple MOU. Keith, the corporate lackey not too long ago, was now officially a "pig," living on the startup edge.

Billion-Dollar Vision

Despite still being a tiny business in a relatively obscure African market, we were starting to attract some international attention. A few months earlier, I had received a cold-call email inviting me to speak on a panel at a social enterprise conference at Columbia Business School in New York. I promptly declined, citing a lack of cash for international travel. Another panelist, Martin Hartigan, replied with an offer to pay my way and put me up in his apartment. Martin had enjoyed a long career at the World Bank, and his wife Pamela had recently — and coincidentally — been appointed as director of Oxford's Skoll Centre for Social Entrepreneurship. He was entirely unaware that I had attended Oxford as a Skoll Scholar; his offer was a simple act of generosity that allowed me to attend the conference.

Finding myself unexpectedly in the U.S., I followed my entrepreneurial instincts and decided to make the most of the opportunity. I flew to San Francisco to attend the Social Capital Markets conference, where I knew many impact investors would be congregating. Unable to afford the conference fee but bolstered with confidence, I sent an email with an offer to make a presentation on Mobile Transactions in exchange for a pass. I got it, along with an invitation to a startup pitching competition hosted by Omidyar Network, an impact investment organization created by eBay founder Pierre Omidyar and his wife Pam.

My pitch didn't win the competition, but it caught the attention of Arjuna Costa, who had recently joined Omidyar

Network to build its emerging markets financial services portfolio. Arjuna invited me to his Silicon Valley office after the conference, where I filled a whiteboard with Mobile Transactions' long-term vision of driving toward a cashless Africa by offering a full suite of digital payments and financial services. I anchored my presentation on the contract we were poised to sign with the World Food Programme (WFP), which would far surpass our fledgling money transfer business and provide a growth path into other markets. He told me to keep in touch and send him more materials so that he could get to know our model better.

I also had dinner with the leadership team of Kiva, a crowdfunding platform that allowed people to make zero-interest loans to micro- and small businesses around the world, entirely at their risk. They were based in San Francisco and were attending the same event. A few months earlier, I had been coincidentally seated next to Kiva's co-founder and CEO Matt Flannery at the 2010 Skoll World Forum in Oxford, where I pitched the idea of a partnership. Then, after an ash cloud from the Eyjafjallajökull volcano in Iceland had grounded all aircraft and stranded us both in London, we serendipitously met up again to hash out the details. Now, Matt and his team confirmed their approval to make Mobile Transactions Kiva's first ever nontraditional micro-finance partner, subject to a due diligence trip in the coming weeks. This would provide us with a renewable source of interest- and risk-free capital to pass on to our champion agents to fund their float and outlet expansion.

My last meeting in the Bay Area was in Mountain View with my Google secret weapon, Patrick Pichette. I was in awe of him, but he kept telling me how envious he was *of me*. Patrick greatly respected that I was an entrepreneur painting a vision onto a blank canvas, and he reinforced the need for us to be bold with our ambition. "To change the world, you need to dream big," he said, sharing stories about the people he worked with who thought this way. Like us, Patrick knew there were billions of people in emerging markets around the world who lacked access to financial services but were rapidly being brought online with the expansion of the internet and mobile phone industry. "Someone is going to provide all those people with financial services," he said. "There is no reason why that can't be you."

The next morning, I flew from San Francisco to Washington, D.C. to meet with Monica Brand-Engel, who was managing the Accion Frontier Investment Group. Accion was a global NGO founded in the 1960s that had played a major role in building the micro-finance industry, and was now making impact investments in payment and financial service startups in emerging markets. Brad had met Monica on a trip to Washington several months earlier, and they had made a mutually enthusiastic connection. I replicated the whiteboard I had drawn for Arjuna, again double-clicking on our pending WFP contract and scaling strategy. Monica was happy enough to offer to organize a due diligence trip to meet our team and see our operations in the field in early 2011.

I ended my trip meeting with John Schroeder, an experienced entrepreneur and venture investor in the U.S. who had previously worked with Monica and was now, coincidentally, the chief investment officer at the GBF. We had met a few months earlier when he visited Lusaka; now John informed me that he was leaving GBF, but offered to help me set up and chair a Mobile Transactions advisory board with the goal of raising a Series A investment round.

On the long plane ride back to Lusaka, I reflected on how much I had learned in one short week, and on the sheer number of people who were supporting and cheering for us. I was both humbled and inspired, and kept thinking back to the conversation I had had with Patrick, in particular, in which he'd challenged me to think big. My heart thumped and my mind raced with excitement and possibility as I thought about how we were pioneering a new startup business model that was poised to achieve real impact at scale.

When the plane landed, I called Brad, Brett and Keith to debrief. "Let's go raise a Series A investment and build a billion-dollar business!" I proclaimed to an enthusiastic audience that was feeding off my positive energy.

The future had never been brighter.

Cash Crunch

It didn't take long to get dragged back down to earth.

At the beginning of December 2010, I met with the World Food Programme project lead in Lusaka to update him on our newfound investor interest, which would support our partnership in Zambia and potential expansion beyond. The draft contract between the WFP and Mobile Transactions had been reviewed and mostly agreed, and I pulled it from my bag not at all prepared for what I was about to hear.

The contract, I discovered to my dismay, would not be signed. The cited reason was a WFP funding crunch due to a banking crisis in Ireland, combined with a recent announcement from the World Bank that officially classified Zambia as a middle-income country, which affected the country's status with donors. That was it, no room to negotiate.

I felt sick to my stomach. Losing that contract was a potential death blow to our hopes of raising investment, and possibly even to our business. This time, when I relayed the news to my

partners, there were no belly laughs from Brett. We all knew
we were in deep trouble. Keith immediately offered to take
a consulting job so that he wouldn't have to draw a salary.
We called John Schroeder, who walked us back from the ledge.
He advised me to immediately notify GBF and our prospective
investors, Accion and Omidyar Network, as they would
welcome the honest and open communication.

After a sleepless weekend, I followed his advice, placing calls
to all three. I appreciated their empathy, particularly from
Monica at Accion, who asked me how she could help. I assured
her we would "make a plan" — which really meant "we'll find
some way out of this mess." We announced to staff that there
would be no "thirteenth check" for Christmas, a customary
bonus in both Zambia and South Africa, and we explained to
some of them that we wouldn't be able to pay their full salaries.
We also called in as many favors as we could, pitching to
people within our network for enterprise payment contracts
and asking them to pay us entirely up front.

I also went back to my personal network and started
scrambling for new investments that could be mobilized
quickly. An EWB friend connected me to Paul Gomes and his
investment partner Joseph Schaefer, based in my hometown
Calgary, who agreed to invest $50,000 of convertible debt. John
stressed that we couldn't just keep asking people to send cash
to our bank account without formal documentation, so we
"hired" Adrian Dommisse — himself a startup lawyer with a
desk in the basement of Brett's neighbor's house — to do the
paperwork. Only we told Adrian we had no money to pay him,
so he took a leap of faith and generously offered to defer all
of his fees until we could close our Series A investment — an
eventuality that was far from certain. He also offered to help us
restructure our original GBF loan, given we could no longer

make the quarterly cash interest payments.

Meanwhile, EWB offered to fly me to their upcoming national conference in Toronto to speak on a panel. I almost declined, but these types of events tend to generate opportunities — in this instance, to meet more angel investors and also to visit the head office of an NGO, the Mennonite Economic Development Associates (MEDA). We had applied for a grant from them some time earlier, but had not heard back.

After giving a presentation to MEDA's staff and learning that the grant was still in process, albeit with uncertain timing, I learned that the NGO had a private investment arm across the street called Sarona Asset Management — another opportunity. Within an hour I had been introduced to Serge LeVert-Chiasson and Gerhard Pries at Sarona, and openly explained our cash-flow predicament caused by the WFP project cancellation just as we were building momentum toward a Series A investment round. After a brief discussion, Gerhard told me that Sarona might be able to help by making a bridge investment out of a reserve of MEDA funds that they managed.

Just two weeks later, Serge landed in Lusaka for a due diligence visit and brought with him a term sheet for a $300,000 convertible debt investment. Of this, $200,000 could be used to completely refinance our GBF loan, which we were negotiating to restructure in light of not being able to afford the quarterly cash interest payments, on better terms. The additional $100,000 would extend our cash runway. This was an amazing offer.

I called GBF and they were pleased to be repaid. They had a positive story to tell about helping launch an innovative startup and exiting to an investor that wanted to support us for the long term. Sarona's investment closed less than a month later, and the MEDA grant came in shortly afterwards. From the verge of bankruptcy in December, we suddenly had, by the end of March 2011, the best-looking cash flow in our history.

Series A

None of Brad, Brett, Keith or I had ever raised an internationally backed Series A investment round before — and we didn't know of any other startup in Africa that had, either. We were very much on the frontier. (There was no such thing as a "Series Seed round" in Africa at the time; today they are commonplace.)

Monica was sending me signals that Accion could move faster than Omidyar Network, so we started with her. She flew to Cape Town to meet Brett and Keith, along with our back-office team of three tech developers, one accountant and two payment processors. Despite having no short-term plans to expand to South Africa, we had decided to create a centralized finance and technology hub in Cape Town, where there was greater access to specialized talent (at lower cost than in Johannesburg). Moreover, we were already thinking about expanding to other African markets with a hub-and-spoke model. In making that call, we now found ourselves on the leading edge of Cape Town's emerging fintech ecosystem, along with Fundamo, a pioneering African payment company that also had a centralized technology office, down the road in the university town of Stellenbosch.

We wanted to pair a global impact investor, such as Accion or Omidyar Network, with a co-investor based in Africa who could help us expand to new markets. While attending an event in Nairobi a couple of months before, I met a contact from my EWB Zambia days who was heading up the East Africa office of AfricInvest, a private equity investor based in Tunisia.

I delivered my Mobile Transactions pitch with senior partner Khaled Ben Jilani dialing in from Tunis, and later followed up by introducing Khaled to Monica over email. They agreed to explore the investment opportunity together, and we all met in Johannesburg for a productive joint meeting that kicked off a formal due diligence process.

The investors asked us to send them a virtual data room that included all company policies and contracts, as well as a financial model projecting out over five years with assumptions about new product and market expansions. Keith took responsibility for preparing the data room, creating everything from scratch — literally, because we had very little written down — based on a long checklist of requested items, while I locked myself in a room for a few weeks to build the financial model, also from scratch. Despite having made it through an Oxford MBA, I had never built such a model before, and this one turned out to be so complicated that we put it on the shelf the day after it was sent to the investors, never making practical use of it. The reality was we were more accustomed to managing a cash-flow forecast that, if we were lucky, stretched three months out.

Meanwhile, an external technology auditor flew in from Tunis to Cape Town to meet Brett. When he asked to review all of the documentation on our system architecture and technology development processes, Brett politely inquired as to the specifics of what he wanted to know, which he would personally outline in detail. After a full day of drawing on the whiteboard, Brett managed to convince the auditor that we had built a secure transaction system with adequate controls in place — we just hadn't written anything down yet.

In reality, we were an overstretched, immature business fighting fires every day. We were learning on the fly what was required to raise institutional capital, and we still had a long way to go.

Firefighting

A week before the Accion and AfricInvest teams were scheduled to land in Lusaka for a market due diligence, we experienced two crises that nearly derailed the entire process.

The first one started at Dunavant, still a 35 percent strategic shareholder in Mobile Transactions at this point, and still using the original payment system Brett had built for them prior to my arrival. They had added value as the original investors behind Brad and Brett's vision, and had sourced more than $400,000 of grant funding from the German Development Agency (DEG) and Next clothing company for our system development and original agent rollout. But we had long shifted our focus away from farmer payments, causing misalignment, and now we learned that Dunavant was being acquired by a much larger commodities company, which put us in limbo. We also knew that Dunavant wasn't planning on investing any more cash, and we were worried that the new owners might not approve of or play nicely with any new shareholders — or vice versa.

We came up with the idea to try to raise a convertible loan that could be used to buy back Dunavant's shares, at cost, allowing them to exit cleanly. This would leave the founders with 100 percent ownership. To fund this buyback, we could offer an investor a good discount into our Series A round since our founder ownership position would be dramatically improved.

The following week, a five-person joint team from Accion and AfricInvest, led by Monica and Khaled, arrived in Lusaka from Washington, D.C. and Tunis, respectively. The Accion team made it without a hitch, but I received a frantic call from

Khaled at Lusaka International Airport. He told me he was being put back on a plane to Johannesburg because we had not provided him a visa to enter Zambia. This was the first I had heard that he even needed a visa, let alone one I was supposed to organize for him. It was a disastrous start to a visit that we were already highly anxious about.

Brad and I realized we had to divide and conquer. He would spend the day taking the other investors around the Lusaka market and on a road trip to the town of Kabwe, two hours' drive away, where we had a high-performing champion agent. Meanwhile, I would figure out how to get Khaled into the country so he could join us for dinner and the second morning before everyone was scheduled to fly on to Cape Town.

After meeting the investors at their hotel and explaining the plan, I drove to Lusaka's central immigration building, a chaotic government office thronged with people queuing in front of desks covered in towering stacks of paper files. I worked my way from desk to desk, and eventually was led upstairs to the private office of the head of immigration for Lusaka. I knew I had to be at my persuasive best, so I pulled out my laptop and walked him through our Mobile Transactions pitch deck. I shared our vision to create jobs for thousands of micro-entrepreneurs while catalyzing a cashless Zambia and bringing millions of dollars of foreign investment into the country — before explaining that this plan was now in jeopardy because our prospective investor had been denied entry into Zambia. The official was swayed and agreed to issue an emergency visa. Much relieved, I relayed the news to Khaled, who booked the next flight to Lusaka. Despite this disruption, the rest of the investors were excited about what they had seen, and they brought Khaled up to speed the next morning. We gave him a quick tour down Cairo Road to visit a couple of champion agents before heading back to the airport in what was a short but eventful visit.

Our guests were equally impressed with our Cape Town team, and when we finally sat down to talk about the investment, I seized on the positive energy to bring up our Dunavant situation, emphasizing both the dilemma and opportunity it presented. Happily, everyone agreed that it was preferable for Dunavant to exit, so that we could start with a clean ownership structure to bring in new investors. I told them how we were hoping to raise convertible debt to buy out Dunavant, and Monica immediately signaled that Accion might be willing to fund this as a show of good faith toward leading our Series A round. We were extremely relieved to hear this news, which she confirmed once she was back in Washington.

We closed the convertible debt investment with Accion, and Dunavant agreed to sell their shares back to the company to settle their initial investment. Dunavant wasn't in the business of venture investing, so they were pleased with this outcome. We were finally ready for a Series A term sheet, which AfricInvest and Accion were promising to give us shortly.

Meanwhile, I kept trying to persuade Arjuna from Omidyar Network to visit us, but he was reluctant to jump in knowing there were other investors much further ahead in the process. I started pitching to other impact investors, and after a European-headquartered global impact investor committed to visiting us, Arjuna's calculus flipped. He would come see us, after all.

Due to travel logistics, I couldn't be in Cape Town when Arjuna started his trip, but Brad, Brett and Keith were ready to go. Keith knew he had limited time to make an impression, so after shaking hands he pulled out his laptop and launched into a presentation of our financials. Arjuna stopped him in his tracks and said he just wanted to have a chat and get to know everyone, a response which Keith read as a strong indicator that we were wasting our time trying to get an investment from Omidyar Network. Brad and Brett, though, lived for telling stories and building relationships, and saw this as a great opportunity. The conversation spilled over to dinner and a few bottles of wine, and afterwards they were buzzing about how much they liked Arjuna and how well the meeting had gone, though Keith was still confused that Arjuna hadn't asked a single financial question. He did, however, appreciate that Arjuna had picked up the bill, as our cash balance was so low at the time that his company bank card would have bounced!

The next day, Arjuna flew to Lusaka to meet me and was joined by an Omidyar Network colleague. They wanted to get outside of the capital city and visit our rural agents, so I organized a trip a few hours north to the rural town of Mkushi. We stopped to meet several agents along the way, and I appreciated how easily Arjuna strolled through markets and seemed to enjoy conversing with traders. When he joined me in eating the traditional Zambian dish of *nshima*, a thickened ball of maize porridge, with his hands, I was convinced he was the right investor for us.

Closing the Deal

In September 2011, Accion and AfricInvest presented us with a joint Series A term sheet for a $2-million investment. This was a huge milestone just over two and half years after I first met Brad and Brett. The pre-money valuation of $4.2-million was lower than we were asking for, but given the equity we had clawed back by exiting Dunavant as a shareholder, we could live with it.

I had never seen an equity term sheet before and there were many things I didn't understand. I scheduled a call with John Schroeder, who congratulated us on the achievement but then walked us through a number of clauses that he felt weren't in our best interests at such an early stage. There were numerous downside protections in favor of the investors, including a steep liquidation preference where, if the company was ever sold, the investors would receive a multiple of their money back before the founders and employees got anything. There were also a number of control terms we didn't like, such as the right of the investors to force a process that could prematurely lead to a sale of the company. I had to go back and negotiate.

Arjuna's term sheet from Omidyar Network arrived shortly after. It was for a $3-million investment at a slightly higher pre-money valuation of $4.5-million, with a more reasonable liquidation preference and no forced exit clause. John confirmed that this term sheet was closer to "plain vanilla" and more in line with what he was expecting at a Series A stage. We really liked Accion and AfricInvest, but comparing the two term sheets, and considering how much we also liked Arjuna, the decision was ultimately an easy one. There was some last-minute drama as Arjuna had to track down Pierre Omidyar himself for a signature, which came minutes before a deadline we had imposed, but we signed with Omidyar Network on October 27, 2011.

I made the difficult phone calls to Monica and Khaled. They were both disappointed, given how much time and effort they had put into the deal and how accommodating they had been to us. As a silver lining, I told them that the Omidyar Network term sheet left room for a co-investor to join for up to $1.5-million of the $3-million round. They both promised to consider it, and a few days later Monica called me to confirm Accion would take up the remaining amount and sign the Omidyar Network term sheet. We were home free — or so we thought — subject to drafting and signing final legal agreements and taking some actions to clean up and simplify our corporate structure.

I was just starting to relax when Brad announced to us all one day that he was moving from Lusaka to the KwaZulu-Natal Midlands in the eastern part of South Africa, where he had once gone to boarding school. He had made the decision without consulting me, and without discussing what impact it could have on our business or the investment round; he simply stated that he was going to set up an office in his house and commute to Zambia whenever he was needed.

Despite the blindside, I knew Brad well enough to understand his rationale. Brad's two teenage daughters were at a girls' boarding school nearby. He and his wife Jill had been flying back and forth to visit them, and then Jill had been diagnosed with skin cancer. She was spending all of her time in South Africa for treatment and to be closer to their girls, and Brad was living alone in Lusaka, stressed, with his daughters and wife far away, on top of the investor, business and cash-flow pressures that we were all dealing with on a day-to-day basis. I also knew that Brad felt strongly that this was his decision to make, and he had no intention of changing his mind.

I pledged to forge ahead, but I was hurt and upset by the position it put me in as the CEO interfacing with our prospective investors. I chose not to disclose this information to Monica and Arjuna, convincing myself that it would be better to ask for forgiveness later rather than permission now.

A week before our Series A deal was scheduled to close, I was on a conference call to go through the final transaction documents with the Accion and Omidyar legal teams and our lawyer, Adrian. Somehow it slipped out that Brad had moved to South Africa, and Arjuna asked me point-blank if it was true. I confirmed that he had, but also that Brad was spending as much time in Zambia as he needed to and that we were all finding this configuration beneficial. Brad's value tended to come in focused bursts, and I had been pleasantly surprised to find myself working more effectively with him now that I had a bit more space in Zambia and his personal life was more stable. I stressed on the call that we were focused on deliverables and results, not where people lived and how many hours they worked.

Monica wasn't on the call, but she phoned me the next day to say she had heard the news and was considering pulling her investment. She was upset by the news itself, but more so that I hadn't disclosed such a material issue earlier, which eroded her trust in both our team and me.

Thankfully, the investors chose to take a leap of faith and proceed. On February 10, 2012 our Series A investment closed with a total round size of $4-million, which consisted of $2.8-million in new cash coming in and $1.2-million of debt converted from previous founder and bridge investments. The debt conversion included some funds advanced from Accion and Sarona after the term sheet was signed to ensure we would get to close.

It felt like the end of a marathon. Keith took a screenshot of our bank statement when the funds cleared, and we all let out a collective exhale. We should have celebrated, but we didn't; we were simply too exhausted. There was, however, much to be proud of. We had closed one of the first meaningful fintech equity investments in Africa, and I had accomplished my original goal of connecting purpose-driven entrepreneurs with global impact investors.

It was now time to refocus our attention back toward our

vision of building a billion-dollar business in pursuit of a cashless Africa.

Becoming Zoona

Before we could get started, though, there was one more big change we needed to make.

The Mobile Transactions brand was hurting us. The name "Mobile Transactions" itself was problematic, and many people simply used "MTZL," the abbreviation for Mobile Transactions Zambia Limited. The multi-color logo with three balls and interconnected arrows meant to depict transaction flows was also complicated and hard for painters to replicate on agent outlets, resulting in many variations across the country. Some consumers we surveyed couldn't even name our company and simply referred to us as "the one with the balls."

We had tried once in 2011 to hastily rebrand as "Makwacha," which meant "more money" in Zambia. However, we prematurely painted the new name on the walls of our Lusaka champion agent outlets without submitting a trademark application — a move that was noticed by the dominant mobile network operator in the market, Zain, which quickly registered a company called Makwacha Limited and sent us a cease-and-desist letter. We then watched as Zain launched an M-Pesa copycat mobile money product branded as Makwacha. Thankfully for us, their product failed to gain traction before Zain was acquired by Airtel, an Indian MNO, which dropped the Makwacha brand as they prepared to launch their own product called "Airtel Money," but we learned an important lesson about protecting our brand assets. This was our first taste of competing with MNOs, and now that we were on their radar we knew it would not be our last.

Returning to first principles, Brad spearheaded a process, supported by a boutique brand agency, to create a new brand identity derived from our core values. We codified these as *being real, entrepreneurship, integrity, togetherness, commitment* and *fun*. We chose to stick with green as our primary color as a symbol of growth (and our agricultural roots), but opted for a brighter shade to make it more eye-catching. We would later add the secondary color blue as a symbol of water, which was plentiful in Zambia with its lakes and rivers, including the Zambezi River and Victoria Falls, along with the huge Lake Malawi next door in the country that would become our second market.

When it came to brainstorming new names, I asked Brad and Brett what they thought about returning to their original choice of "Zoona," given that it was the literal translation of our core value of "being real." Isabelle and I had liked the word so much we had given it as a name to our new German Shepherd puppy. It turned out they were thinking the same thing, so we made the decision on the spot. Zoona as a brand was born again, sealed with a new logo that consisted of a "Z" embedded in a speech bubble to symbolize our word-of-mouth spread.

We were ready. We had $2.8-million of cash in the bank and a clear path ahead. Surely nothing could stop us now.

PART 2: FAILING

"You may encounter many defeats,
but you must not be defeated. In fact, it may
be necessary to encounter the defeats,
so you can know who you are, what you can
rise from, how you can still come out of it."
— MAYA ANGELOU

CHAPTER 3

FAILING TO BECOME A TEAM

In the long lead-up to our Series A investment closing — a full three and a half years after I landed in Lusaka — Brad, Brett, Keith and I were all too busy just trying to survive to worry about how we were working together. With fresh money in the bank, we might have anticipated a time of jovial relaxation ahead, but the period that followed was nothing of the sort; instead, we found our many underlying and undealt-with issues come welling to the surface. We were thrust into seemingly constant conflict that consumed a huge amount of time and energy, and came close to breaking us on several occasions. Our only chance for survival was to figure out how to become a team.

Our problematic co-founder dynamics had been brewing for some time, dating back to January 2010 when Isabelle and I returned to Lusaka after a two-week honeymoon in Mali. We had trekked to Timbuktu to attend the Festival au Désert, an eclectic music festival in the Sahara desert, and on arriving back at the Mobile Transactions office I was relaxed, happy and ready to take on the world. After the welcome-home pleasantries, Brad told me I was now officially the general manager of Mobile Transactions Zambia and ticked off the top agenda item on his notepad. He believed I could do better than him at implementing the necessary day-to-day structures that we needed to scale, while he was elevated to a more strategic level as an executive director and shareholder.

Brad and I were joined at the hip most days, and I knew his intentions were to pull me closer to the core and feed my ambition, since I was technically still a paid consultant for the Grassroots Business Fund at that point. It was a genuine act of humility and a huge vote of confidence — but nothing really changed afterwards. Brett remained the managing director of the holding company that owned our technology and intellectual property, while Brad and I kept working together to grow our fledgling champion agent network.

Six months later, Brad flew to Washington, D.C. to attend a GBF event. He met several impact investors and heard first-hand how much the gesture of passing the general manager torch to me in Zambia, and offering me sweat equity with it, had reverberated in that small circle. It was seen by investors as unusual for a founder to be willing to cede some control to an outside "professional" (a silly heuristic my Oxford MBA brought with it). For better or for worse, this perception seemed to outweigh the fact that Brad was more than a decade older than me, with years of entrepreneurial experience in Africa under his belt. In reality I was merely the apprentice.

Being a pragmatist, Brad then came to the conclusion that we needed one CEO to access more capital from the predominantly American impact investors we were coveting, but if he or Brett assumed the title, Mobile Transactions would always be perceived by that audience as a family business. It was also untenable to have multiple CEOs, as our current structure suggested. So the first thing Brad did when he returned from

Washington was inform me that I was now the CEO of the Mobile Transactions "group" of companies, including the holding entity.

This turned out to be neither a true promotion nor a smooth transition, most evident when I found out that Brad hadn't consulted Brett. "When the hell did Mike become the CEO?" Brett asked during an argument several weeks later. Brad told me not to worry, figuring that his brother would eventually get on board, which he did. As angry as he could get at times, Brett ultimately trusted Brad's instincts, which were often spot on. Besides, when the dust settled, nothing much had changed other than my title, and we tried to carry on as if everything else was the same as before.

Making Decisions

While the CEO title did serve to formalize my role externally and accentuated the narrative of the founding brothers being serious about building an "investible business," internally things were more complicated. Brad and Brett were the original founders and the owners of the majority of the company's equity; they were older than me and they had launched multiple startups together. On top of this, they were brothers born in Zambia and often seemed to communicate by telepathy. It didn't matter that I was called "CEO" — I was still very much an outsider, and for a long time a third wheel. Keith's arrival in October 2010 helped to provide a counterweight, but it also frequently created "us versus them" positions, which ultimately made it clear that the real power lay with Brad and Brett. Moreover, Keith had left investment banking on the premise of being able to make his own decisions and not have to answer to a boss, let alone one who was his friend.

Any naive vision I may have started with of the CEO making "the big decisions" was thus quickly scrubbed and replaced with the more modest goal of simply achieving and maintaining harmony among our founding team. For months this was a challenge I failed on a daily basis. Even the smallest decisions required the full buy-in of all four of us, and were guaranteed to cause repetitive loops of conflict across both our Cape Town and Lusaka offices while our staff went about their business pretending not to notice. Often, our arguments were carried out over email, with us yelling at each other as loud as we could type, resorting to ALL CAPS as the situation deteriorated, until finally the issue would boil over and we would hold an emergency Skype voice call. By then, none of us could remember what the original disagreement was about, and once we stopped and listened to each other we would realize we were generally aligned. Eventually, we created a code word — "Mango" — that anyone could use to stop the email bloodshed and shift to an urgent founder Skype call before things spiraled further. (There wasn't enough internet bandwidth in Lusaka at the time to make video calls. By comparison, today's Zoom meetings, in which you can actually see the people you are talking to, seem like a dream!)

Gradually, I learned to stop asserting what I thought was right and just focused on trying to achieve alignment. I also deliberately changed my mindset to become an enabler of Brad and Brett as the original founders, and over time Keith as CFO; I figured that whatever aligned position I could facilitate on an issue would be better than a position that any one person disagreed with, which would likely face sabotage during implementation as a result. This shift in approach defused team conflict and allowed us to keep moving forward, even when decisions were suboptimal. Eventually, Brad, Brett and

Keith grew to trust that whatever position I took as CEO was an amalgamation of theirs, and I grew more skilled at finding the common ground and teasing out hidden differences for discussion. Our decision-making pace improved, as did the quality of our decisions and subsequent implementation.

This was hard, exhausting work, which frequently left me burnt out, questioning myself and seeking counselling from my wife after hours. Then, just as I was getting the hang of it, everything got harder again after our Series A investment.

Thumbs Up

In the months preceding the close of our Series A, I started to deliberately position my role to investors as "CEO" instead of "co-founder." Neither our investors nor Brad or Brett could quite figure out where to place me in the investor versus founder negotiation, and at times I didn't really know myself. What was clear to me was that I could appreciate each side's perspective on most issues better than either could of the other. So, I signaled to everyone that my role was to act as a bridge and find compromises to entrenched positions, of which there were several. One was founder compensation.

From the outset, the four of us as founders had received identical salaries, with Keith and me accruing a portion as sweat equity until Series A. In our first post-investment board meeting, however, our board formed an HR subcommittee that immediately flagged this as an issue, with a suggestion that we shift to differentiated compensation based on roles. To the subcommittee, in which Brad as the founder representative was outnumbered by Monica as an investor and John as an independent, this was in line with best practice and a sign of founder maturity. To Brad and Brett, the implication was that

Keith and I should get paid more than them, and that their years of entrepreneurial (not to mention life) experience were perceived as being worth less than our Oxford MBAs. Keith and I had no qualms about equal salaries, and never would have dared to suggest otherwise, because we understood the conflict and misalignment it would instantly create — which is exactly what happened.

As with most emotive issues, I personally absorbed the conflict, feeling as if all fingers were pointed at me as the cause. Was I on a power trip to diminish Brad and Brett and align with our new investors, while secretly lobbying for a pay raise? Or was I a lame duck CEO wasting investor cash on founder salaries because I lacked the maturity to make rational, evidence-based decisions based on "best practice"? As the issue snowballed, I felt the pressure build on me to find a solution.

Since differentiated founder compensation was nothing any of us had asked for or wanted, I pushed back and convinced the board to keep it the way it was. We retained this precedent throughout my tenure and it worked well for us, signaling to each other and everyone else that despite our titles, we were all of equal value to the business. Eventually, it would also become a non-issue to our board, especially after our financial results spoke for themselves.

Another board-instigated challenge came when our principle of collective decision-making was questioned. I brought this up casually at a board meeting one day, without anticipating any pushback. Instead, it lit a fire where I again found myself being harangued by my co-founders on one side, who were looking at me to align everyone on "*our* way of working," and certain board members on the other side who were adamant that the CEO should be the decision-maker. The debate ended without resolution and with mass frustration, and spilt over in assorted post-meeting lobbying efforts to convince me why our approach was either right or wrong.

I took this decision-making challenge to my dad. In addition to being a career high-school teacher, he was also four-time president of Canada's largest teachers' association and had seen his fair share of contentious negotiations. After retiring, he completed a master's in alternative approaches to conflict resolution and started a private consultancy in Canada's education sector, helping deeply entrenched sides come together to find solutions.

My dad shared with me the counterintuitive insight that consensus decision-making doesn't require everyone to agree with the decision — it just requires getting everyone *comfortable enough* to move forward. He walked me through a very simple framework that he had found effective with much larger groups and far more emotionally charged issues. When making a decision, each person is given the opportunity to vote thumbs-up, thumbs-down or thumbs-neutral. Those who vote thumbs-down have to voice their concerns while the others listen. The group then brainstorms ways to address those concerns in order to get the dissenters to move at least to thumbs-neutral without the compromise shifting anyone else to thumbs-down. Once everyone is thumbs-up or thumbs-neutral, the decision is made and documented, with a commitment to move forward as a group. No one is allowed to backtrack and all side conversations are quashed.

Out of our discussion, I created a document that I presented to our board called "Mike's Leadership Principles." In it, I declared that my first-order priority as CEO was to achieve alignment and build consensus among and between our founding team and board, while remaining accountable, as CEO, for any and all outcomes. I included my dad's thumbs-up, thumbs-neutral and thumbs-down framework to enshrine decision-making, stressing that this was how I intended to make decisions. Our board formally endorsed my leadership principles with a thumbs-up vote, and from that day forward we never made a material decision as founding team or board where someone remained "thumbs-down."

Performance Management

With money in the bank and heightened expectations, the pressure to deliver increased dramatically. All of us felt this, but Keith was the first to show signs of cracking.

For the previous 18 months, Keith had done a heroic job managing our cash flow and holding together the pieces of our back-end finance system. As our accounting workload increased, Keith responded the way he always had — by rolling up his sleeves and working harder, late into the nights and through weekends. He exuded stress as he sat hunched over his laptop with his head in his hands, or marching as fast as he could, at the same time every day, to the downstairs pizza takeaway for lunch to minimize the minutes away from his desk. He would reject meeting requests and abruptly end conversations, saying he was too busy. Finding a moment to discuss strategy with him was near-impossible.

Brad, Brett and I agreed we needed an intervention, and we convinced Keith that with money in the bank he needed to hire help. Luckily, he proved to be a masterful talent magnet. Among his first recruits was Lelemba Phiri, a Zambian living in Cape Town with an accounting certification — something Keith didn't have — and an entrepreneurial side hustle helping people manage their personal finances. Keith convinced Lelemba that Zoona could be a long-term home for her to pursue her passion for developing young African talent, while also filling our immediate need for a finance manager reporting to him.

Even with Lelemba on board, though, Keith still struggled to pull himself out of the weeds. He was reluctant to delegate and I became concerned that Lelemba would resign for lack of responsibility, so I summoned the courage to tell Keith that the current arrangement wasn't working. I told him bluntly that I was shifting Lelemba to report directly to me, with everyone else on our finance team reporting to her, while Keith took a break. I also told him I was removing his CFO title, and that we would have to define a new role for him when he got back.

Keith was surprised and upset at the intervention, but he was aware that he was sinking. He took off to go surfing for a couple of weeks, which proved to be a helpful break for everyone and enabled Lelemba to quickly assume his finance responsibilities. But while Keith returned refreshed, he was lost without a role or title.

Over lunch one day, the two of us came up with a new role for him: He would be responsible for special projects that were strategic to the business, starting with building a new working capital credit model that we thought we needed to scale up the float we were extending to our agents. I sent Keith off to work alone and he returned a few weeks later having created a masterpiece — the only problem being, as I explained to him, that his model was far more complex than what we needed at the time and had little practical value.

Meanwhile, I instituted a quarterly performance appraisal process in an attempt to create more formal accountability. I started with Brad and Brett, who scored themselves a four out of five on their recent work, while I gave them each a three. They weren't happy, but I justified it to them as wanting to set a high bar. I scored Keith two out five, piling on the hurt I had already caused when I stripped him of his CFO role and then informed him that his first project in his new role was a failure. I also scored Lelemba a two out of five after her first quarter reporting to me, rationalizing that she was new to the role and had a long way to go to get to the executive leadership level that I expected.

My very first individual performance appraisals were completely rational — and also completely blind to their emotional impact. I angered Brad and Brett, kicked Keith when he was already down and encouraged our first senior hire to consider quitting. I had asserted myself as CEO, but demoralized everyone in the process.

Help from Afar

I clearly needed help. Arjuna introduced me to Susan Phillips at Omidyar Network, a coach on their human capital team. After a few phone discussions about my daily dilemmas and emotionally draining conflicts with our executive team, Susan offered to fly to Cape Town and run a pro bono team-building workshop for us. I gratefully accepted.

Before the workshop, Susan asked us to complete a Myers-Briggs personality indicator test, the results of which she then handed to us in person. She explained how Myers-Briggs would reveal our personality preferences, which are akin to being left-handed or right-handed. They are not path-determinant, but rather preferences established at a young age that can be generalized to predict behavior patterns in certain situations.

The results were illuminating. Brad and I were both extroverts, with strong "intuition," which explained our ability to see the bigger picture and take great leaps of faith. Brett, also an extrovert, had a "sensing," as opposed to intuitive, preference, which made him more attuned to details than Brad and I. Keith was an introvert, which helped explain how exhausting it was for him to work with us. As extroverts, we generated energy and ideas through constant verbal brainstorming. Keith needed time and space to think. For the first time we understood his reluctance to take off his headphones and engage with us whenever we beckoned.

All four founders had a preference for "perceiving," which is roughly synonymous with spontaneity, and this accounted for how naturally effective we were at handling crises; we could change directions easily and adapt to the situation. Yet we all struggled with situations that called for order and stability. Lelemba was the opposite, with a "judging" preference and a propensity for planning, which was a helpful counterbalance. Susan also noted that we all had a strong preference for "thinking" instead of "feeling" when it came to decision-making, which meant we would naturally make rational decisions but would have a collective blind spot when considering the effects of decisions on other people.

Susan followed this personality discussion with an assessment of our individual strengths, weaknesses and blind spots. It was enlightening for each of us to learn about ourselves, with the value compounding once we started to learn about each other. Susan effectively brought to light how different combinations of our team could be optimally paired to accomplish certain tasks, while highlighting missing skill sets that we would have to find elsewhere.

This workshop was a game-changer for our team. We ended with a dramatically improved understanding of ourselves and each other. Keith in particular was deeply affected by the realization that the repetitive finance tasks he had previously poured all of his time and effort into were not well-matched to his personal preferences or strengths; they had drained all of his energy while locking him into a downward spiral of declining performance. As an introvert, he internalized these challenges rather than sharing them, thus growing further apart from the rest of us.

Personally, I became much more aware of my blind spot for prioritizing "thinking" over "feeling" when making decisions, which explained a lot of the turmoil I had caused when executing Keith's role shift and my first attempt at team performance appraisals. I also had a much greater appreciation for the differences between extroverts and introverts, and how I specifically needed to adjust my own behavior to create more space for Keith to re-energize, while checking in with him more frequently to better understand what he was working on.

Center of Gravity

A year after our Series A closed, I came to the realization that I needed to move from Lusaka to Cape Town in order to make the full transition to CEO and leader of our team. We were burning through cash quickly without ever being fully aligned on anything, and too much of our team conflict was rooted in poor communication exacerbated by distance. Plus, I was the only one in Zambia, with Brett, Keith and Lelemba based in Cape Town, and Brad spending more time there. Too often, I was left out of important discussions while remaining bogged down in Zambian administrative details and struggling through patchy Skype calls that would frequently drop.

I proposed that Lelemba swap with me and move to Lusaka to become our Zambia managing director. This was a leadership role more in line with her strengths of managing execution and growing people, which aligned with her career ambition of becoming a business leader. Plus, she was Zambian, with a great network, and was keen to return home.

On proposing this shift to our board, I was met with some skepticism about my motive. It was only a year since Brad's move to KwaZulu-Natal to be with his family, and Isabelle and I had just had our first child. Was I really serious about building a billion-dollar business or was I looking to enjoy a more relaxed family lifestyle in Cape Town? Wouldn't it be better for the business if I stayed in Lusaka, instead joined by Brad, Brett and Keith so we could all be closer to our customers and front-line staff?

These were legitimate questions. But I also felt my decision was the right one for our team and business. We had already designed our shared-services fintech hub in Cape Town for multi-country scale, and we were confident Lelemba would do a better job running our Zambia business than any of us.

After a lengthy and somewhat emotive debate, it was the voice of our independent board member, Justin Stanford, that carried the day. As he put it, "The CEO should be based at the business's center of gravity, and in this case I believe it has already shifted to Cape Town." His observation was spot on and it proved to be the correct call.

After Lelemba took over as managing director, the positive results came quickly. In nearly four years since starting, we had built up 119 agent outlets; Lelemba doubled that within her first 12 months. Meanwhile, the conflict between the founder team was reduced dramatically, and we started getting things done faster and better. I set up my desk next to Brett and began working closely with him to better understand how our systems worked and pull our product roadmap out of his head. Keith and I rebuilt our working relationship, which led to his re-emergence as our CFO. He would go on to spearhead a brand-new data function, build off that momentum to take over finance again, and later add legal, risk and regulation. He also earned the trust of our board and became my close partner in all future fundraising rounds.

As I grew as a leader, Brad and Brett also grew to accept and respect my CEO role. In one defining conversation, they made it explicit that although we had different management roles in the business, all four of us were co-founders together. We committed to each other that it was time to realign our individual and team behaviors to stop fighting with each other and instead focus on growing the pie as large as possible to achieve the impact and commercial success we all now believed was possible.

I also developed an improved performance management process, with both team and individual objectives transparently discussed and *agreed up front*, with clear scoring criteria. We learned how to give each other honest and real-time feedback when issues arose so that they wouldn't fester. At performance-appraisal time, everyone knew where they stood, and appraisal meetings became positive conversations about opportunities for improvement and growth.

For the first time, I started to feel like I was becoming a CEO, and we were becoming a team. In fact, we would become a *great* team.

EMBRACING FAILURE: LESSONS LEARNED

There is an African proverb: "As the elephants fight, the grass suffers." When I look back, I shudder at how much time and emotional strain it took for our founding team to come together and work as a team, at great expense to our business. Founders set the vision and are the renewable source of energy in a startup, so if they are fighting or misaligned, the probability of failure — and founder burnout — will spike. It doesn't need to be this way.

A better path starts by recognizing that founders will spend as much time with each other as they will with their partners and families over the life of a startup — possibly more. From that understanding, taking deliberate steps to "become a team" is a first-order priority. This is more than just about achieving harmony, as was my mindset for a long time; it is about becoming an aligned, high-performing team that scales with the business.

Before committing to a new project or startup, I would start with a thorough and upfront vetting of who to work with as co-founders. This would involve a series of honest conversations to surface commonality and differences in values, motivations, risk tolerances, personalities, strengths, weaknesses and blind spots. Taking tests like Myers-Briggs, Gallup's StrengthsFinder and Enneagram — all of which we ended up using — and discussing the results together can be very helpful, as can having conversations with people who have worked with the potential co-founders before. These steps can occur over a structured "dating process" before committing, with built-in off-ramps if it doesn't work out; for example, when agreeing founder equity splits, apply a vesting period (four years is standard) that starts vesting after a 12-month "cliff" to ensure the relationship is an enduring one.

When the founding team gets going, I would take time to create roles that fit the skills, experiences and passions of each founder, and review these regularly as the business changes and grows. Founders often get stuck doing things they don't like or aren't good at because there's nobody else to do them; this can be counterproductive and drain energy, so it's better to be explicit about where the gaps are and try to fill them in other ways. It's also important to have frequent honest conversations that bring to the surface and address underlying issues, and not let anything fester or go unsaid. Good communication is a bedrock for building trust and relationships; it should be prioritized.

When it comes to making decisions, I would establish a clear decision-making framework that gives everyone a voice and encourages debate and disagreement, but makes it clear that a decision means we move forward together. Voting with thumbs worked for us, with the expectation that a thumbs-neutral vote was an agreement to commit to the decision without looking back or assigning blame if it didn't work out. It is more important to make a wrong decision that you reflect on and learn from than delay or avoid making a decision at all.

Even with these actions, success is never guaranteed. Any founding team will undoubtedly go through difficult periods, which may even result in a founder exiting. Skilled external coaching and facilitation can be very helpful in both minimizing these downsides and helping the team get through to the other side when they occur. What matters most is being honest when things aren't working, and purposeful about becoming better.

CHAPTER 4

FAILING TO MANAGE A BOARD

From the day we closed our Series A investment, I suddenly found myself with the new responsibility of having to manage a formal board — a responsibility I wholly underestimated. I had expected instant strategic value and direction from the first meeting; instead I found a new source of anxiety and stress that paralleled my rocky path to becoming a co-founder and CEO. I also quickly realized how much time and energy it was consuming, with no clear return on investment.

Much of this — though not all of it — was due to my complete lack of board experience other than a few virtual advisory board calls. During our Series A negotiation, it became a non-negotiable that Omidyar Network and Accion, as co-lead investors, would each have a voting board seat. It was also a non-negotiable that they would not accept the founders controlling a majority of the board votes; meanwhile, Brad and Brett argued the exact same thing in reverse. Both sides agreed that I, as CEO, should have a voting board seat, but in the eyes of the investors I was more aligned with the founders and would therefore tip the scale in their direction. To break the impasse, we settled on a neutral board with seven voting directors: Arjuna (Omidyar Network), Monica (Accion), Brad, Brett and me, plus two independents. I proposed that the first independent director (and board chair) should be our helpful advisor, John Schroeder. He had previously worked with Monica and had good relationships with everyone, so all were supportive. We agreed that the second independent director would be recruited as soon as possible and would require mutual consent from both founders and investors.

A seven-person board for a fledgling Series A company with a first-time CEO is, in hindsight, way too big — but there was even more to it than that. Sarona, which had converted its debt into Series A equity, also insisted on having a non-voting observer who would attend all board meetings. For the role they nominated Donovan Nickel, a former Hewlett Packard executive and current board member of MEDA, the NGO affiliated with Sarona and technically our shareholder. To counter this, we insisted that Keith be granted the same non-voting observer status, given his role as CFO and member of our founding team. Nobody wanted to write up the board minutes, so we appointed our lawyer, Adrian Dommisse, as board secretary; he even agreed to do this pro bono, after we settled his long-deferred legal bill.

This *might* have been manageable had we all been in the same place to see each other often, but that wasn't the case. When they weren't on airplanes, which seemed to be most of the time, Arjuna and Monica were based in Silicon Valley and Washington, D.C. respectively. John was also in Washington and Donovan was in Boulder, Colorado. It was challenging enough to organize a voice call over a clean line that didn't drop every few minutes, let alone finding mutual availability across several time zones. On top of that, our board had very limited market understanding of Zambia, and since we were

Omidyar Network and Accion's first fintech investment in Africa, everyone was learning on the fly.

To build camaraderie and connection, we agreed that we would hold quarterly in-person board meetings, either in Lusaka or Cape Town, along with monthly board calls. The admin that went into organizing the in-person meetings was non-trivial for everyone given the travel involved, and diverted a lot of my time away from preparing for the actual meetings to the equally challenging objective of making sure everyone just arrived — which was never guaranteed. For one board meeting, in Lusaka in 2013, Monica had a flight hiccup in Washington, and couldn't make her connecting flight from Johannesburg until it was too late. Rather than returning on the transatlantic flight back home, she ended up flying to Cape Town — the day after Brad, Brett and I had flown from Cape Town to Lusaka — while we scrambled to secure one of Lusaka's first fiber internet connections to host a video call in a shared office space. In my haste, I failed to enquire about the cost and almost had a heart attack when we later received an invoice for $8,000 for bandwidth usage! That may have been our most expensive board meeting logistics error, but it certainly wasn't the only one.

"I Don't Do Board Calls"

As CEO, the recruitment of the second independent director technically fell in my court. Since I had no idea where to even start, I was offered pro bono support from Omidyar Network's human capital team in Silicon Valley, who helped me map out a role and ideal candidate profile, and generate a list of potential candidates. The board unanimously agreed that the vacant seat should be filled by an experienced African entrepreneur, ideally one who had scaled a startup in Africa. Brad, Brett, Keith and I felt that we knew the Zambian market well enough to allow us to search for entrepreneurs from other markets, as long as they could help us scale up.

As I got to work, Brett contacted a former colleague who introduced him to Peter Brown, a prominent South African entrepreneur. Before even meeting him, Brad and Brett seemed convinced that Peter would be a great "founder-friendly" director and that the search was over. He did indeed have a good profile on paper, but I could sense my process becoming derailed before it had even started.

Brett set up a meeting with Peter, so I flew to Cape Town to join them for lunch in the town of Stellenbosch, where Peter lived and worked. He came across as a friendly, smart guy bursting with confidence and vision. He told us that he loved the business we were building, but despised governance. This made him even more attractive to Brett, and by proxy Brad. To avoid a fight I jumped on the bandwagon. We invited Peter to observe our next board meeting as a trial, which we would organize in Cape Town to make it easy for him to attend.

News of our hasty invitation was not particularly well received during the next board call, given that we had arranged it without any discussion or engagement with the non-executive members (John and Monica) of our newly formed HR subcommittee (the third member being Brad). Things became testy as several board members dug into their positions, which became more entrenched in the days after the call. Once again, I felt my stomach tangling itself in knots as I was caught in the middle between my co-founders and the distant non-executives on my board.

The evening before the subsequent board meeting in Cape Town, I arranged for Peter to finally meet with our HR subcommittee for a drink, hoping to break the ice. The first sign of trouble came when John had a passport complication that caused him to push back his flight by a day. So I went with Monica and Brad. Peter pulled up on his motorcycle and greeted us at our table outside Mitchell's Waterfront Brewery, a popular downtown pub. After a round of casual introductions, Monica thanked Peter for his interest in joining our board. She started describing the commitment we were looking for, stressing mandatory participation in quarterly in-person board meetings and monthly board calls. Peter interrupted her.

"Sorry, Monica, I don't do board calls."

Monica carried on. She explained that the monthly board calls were important to build relationships and a shared understanding among board members, especially with everyone scattered around the world.

Peter was, to say the least, unmoved. "Monica," he said casually, "with all due respect I would rather staple my balls to a plank than have to sit on a monthly board call."

Relaxed in his leather jacket, Peter watched Monica and me as our jaws dropped. Brad nervously steered the conversation to a new topic, asking Peter if he could share his many entrepreneurial achievements and his vision for Africa. The ice-breaker hadn't turned out quite how I'd hoped.

At the board meeting the next morning, John formally opened the proceedings and I began by presenting our results, followed by our strategy. Two hours into the all-day meeting, Peter, whose attention had increasingly shifted away from the room, interrupted me and asked, "Who's in charge here? Who is the CEO?" I put my hand up awkwardly. "You have an interesting business that has potential," he said, "but I don't fully understand what you do and what your strategy is. I'm sorry, everyone, I have to go now. Mike, come with me."

There were blank, bewildered faces staring at us as I escorted Peter to the door.

I assumed I was escorting him only that far, but he asked me to walk with him to a shopping center next door, as he had some things to buy. In a health food store, while he read the labels on baby food jars, he told me, "What you are building is interesting but I am not who you need on that board. I hate this governance crap and you already have way too many people in the room. What you need is someone who can help remove all this distraction so you can get on with building your business."

I stood with Peter at the checkout counter as he paid for his baby food, said goodbye, and then walked back to the meeting, where everyone was quietly chatting, waiting for my return. I told them where I had been, and Brad said with a huge, sheepish grin, "Well, I guess he's not the right fit for us after all!" Everyone broke out in hysterical laughter as the tension was swept out from the room.

Try, Try Again

The next day, Peter sent an email introducing me to Justin Stanford, "one of South Africa's pioneering tech entrepreneurs," as he put it. Justin had co-founded a leading internet security software company, a tech startup industry organization and an early-stage venture capital fund. "Justin is the guy you need," wrote Peter.

This time we went through the process properly. I presented Justin's profile to our HR subcommittee, alongside the ideal candidate profile we had earlier developed to highlight where it overlapped and where it didn't. I then set up a call with Justin and the subcommittee, which gave me the green light to invite him to our next board meeting as a trial. Justin was engaged throughout the meeting and shared several insightful comments, including constructive feedback about streamlining board meetings and reducing our governance load. He knew how to speak the language of investors *and* founders because he had been both. Peter was right: Justin was the guy we needed. The board unanimously approved his appointment and he would, in time, become one of my most trusted advisors.

I thought I was done recruiting board members, but it wasn't long before John Schroeder notified me that he would be stepping off our board due to the quarterly travel burden from Washington. With one failed and one successful independent director recruitment under my belt, I felt I was getting the hang of things. I prepared a detailed role profile outlining the board chair responsibilities, the required commitment and the domain expertise we were looking for. Referring back to the original candidate list, I found Charles Niehaus's profile. Charles had recently left Visa, where he had been general manager for Africa and had had a front row seat for Visa's recent $110-million acquisition of the payment company Fundamo, our fellow Cape Town-based fintech pioneer. He expressed interest in the role when I pitched it to him, and he impressed our HR subcommittee on a further vetting call. We invited him to our next meeting, where his domain knowledge filled some crucial gaps in the conversation, and he was unanimously approved to join our board as chair.

Board Dysfunction

With our board finally filled out, I struggled with the assumption that my role was to serve them, rather than the other way around. Technically, I was correct that the CEO reports to the board and the board's ultimate responsibility is to hire and fire the CEO. But in a startup with high growth potential, the real function of the board is to support the founding team to scale up the business in pursuit of *their* vision — through strategic advice, helpful introductions and important cautions to avoid common pitfalls.

For our first few board meetings, none of us yet held this enlightened view. Instead, our board meetings were verbose management updates and efforts to impress the board, rather than meaningful discussion on strategy. They also took up a lot of time, largely due to my inexperience.

Two weeks before a board meeting, I would clear my schedule and spend several days at my desk preparing a "board pack." I didn't know what was meant to go in a board pack, so I defaulted toward a "shock and awe" set of materials that outlined everything we had done, were doing and were thinking of doing. Since I wanted to free Brad, Brett and Keith from this burden — which they gladly saw as mine — to keep them focused on running the business, I would prepare all the materials myself. At our first meeting, I printed them out and bound them for everyone, which proved to be an expensive hassle that nobody appreciated; all the packs were left behind to be shredded when the meeting was done.

For subsequent meetings, I uploaded the board pack virtually into a shared Dropbox folder, always under duress after missing self-imposed deadlines that I had previously communicated to everyone. Often these deadlines were missed due to our founding team cycling through the materials to get aligned, worried that I might be sharing too much about our problems (of which there were always many) or framing things in a way that made us look worse than we needed to. It was always a great relief when I finally uploaded the last of the materials, expecting everyone to review them all in detail before the meeting. Of course, this was not always the case, sometimes because of the sheer size of my board packs, sometimes because of the lateness of my submission, and sometimes because of the unpreparedness of others. (One unexpected upshot of uploading board packs to Dropbox was that I had a good idea, from the app notification log-on alerts, of who was or wasn't prepared for meetings.)

Following advice from John, I would also try to schedule one-on-one calls with board members before meetings to "get their temperature" and pick up on contentious issues; given the size of our board, there was never a shortage of these in early meetings. Rather than help me prepare, though, these calls would leave me with increased anxiety, as they provided a taste of the battles to come — and it was a feeling that would crescendo after relaying the warning signs back to my team, accentuating the ever-present "us versus them" postures.

One of the things I got right was organizing board dinners the night before meetings. These dinners gave everyone a chance to find their feet after long flights and reconnect with the others. They became critically important for building relationships, and would lead to great conversations over wine late into the evening, which would often generate more value for the company than whatever we discussed the following day. When travel glitches led to board members missing the dinner or it being delayed until after the meeting, it always degraded the quality of the meeting itself and wasted time bringing everyone up to speed.

To avoid the distracting bustle of our office, we made a practice of renting external meeting rooms that could comfortably accommodate our large group. Because we were cost-conscious, I jumped at the opportunity to secure a complimentary meeting room at a boutique hotel in Cape Town as a package deal in exchange for our international directors staying there. Their "boardroom" ended up being a makeshift conversion of space adjacent to the reception, with walls filled with artwork of naked women. We ended up holding several meetings in this location — due to its affordability, not its art — and our group would arrive in a full spectrum of dress code. Our observer, Donovan, preferred a formal suit and tie that rather clashed with both the group and the setting, while Brad and Brett never wavered from their standard uniform: Shorts and flip flops. I started off dressing somewhere in the middle, but gradually became more casual as time went on.

We started our full-day agendas by breaking into two subcommittees for Human Resources and Risk and Audit. After we reconvened as a group, the chair would formally open the meeting and then everyone would stare at me. Feeling the weight of expectations, I would talk for two hours straight to present our results and everything we were working on. We would break for lunch, and then I would talk for another two hours to cycle through a laundry list of strategic opportunities while our jet-lagged board members pounded back coffee and did their best to keep their eyes open (not always successfully). Then we would take an hour to summarize what the subcommittees had discussed — a time when, finally, I could be silent — before closing the meeting and saying goodbye to our non-executives, who would then rush back to the airport.

The problem with this format was that there was no time for strategic discussion, and everyone was left frustrated with the (non) outcomes. I did almost all of the talking, and the vast majority of the meeting was a verbal presentation of everything I had included in the board pack. There was limited opportunity for anyone to engage or add value, and whenever anyone tried, their contribution was often met with a defensive rebuke of some form, a symptom of our "us versus them" postures at the time. There would also inevitably be a question or comment that would send my presentation off the rails and spiral the conversation downward. It was as if we were still stuck in the Series A negotiation and due diligence process, rather than everyone pulling together on the same team.

I felt the pressure to fix things but I didn't know how, and I found I was running these meetings just trying to get through them, rather than trying to gain value from them.

The Right Hat

Having observed our dysfunction in his trial meeting, Justin pulled me aside afterwards and offered me some valuable insight. My role as CEO, he explained, was to manage the board in the same way I would have to manage our leadership team. It would take time, but it was worth the investment to get it right; first, to get the board off my back; and second, to gain real value that could help me and the business. He set me the challenge of shortening our meeting agendas to half-days to keep them focused, while cutting back on management updates to allow more time for discussion.

With this advice, I started to take ownership of crafting the meeting agenda. I spent time thinking about what I wanted to get out of the meeting, and cycling through a draft agenda with everyone in advance before aligning with Charles as board chair. My board packs slimmed down, albeit never enough, and improved in quality, and I learned to present in shorter bursts and end with questions to frame discussion topics. Eventually, I started measuring how well I was doing by comparing the percentage of meeting time I spent listening versus talking.

I also addressed a core issue that was feeding our dysfunction: Our board was loaded with conflicting roles. For example, Brad and Brett were simultaneously shareholders, directors and managers who reported to me, not to mention founders and brothers. Monica and Arjuna were directors and also employees of our largest investors. No wonder our early board meetings were a mess: Everyone showed up wearing the wrong hat. We discussed this openly and vowed to improve, after which I introduced the symbolic practice of starting each meeting by asking everyone to leave their baggage at the door, take off whatever hat they were wearing when they came in and put on their Zoona director's hat for the meeting.

As is almost always the case, with enough practice we eventually figured it out. I started to fix board dates and locations a year in advance, hired an assistant to help with logistics, and steadily improved at streamlining board packs and agendas. I prioritized relationship-building by scheduling offsite dinners and activities, such as hiking and ziplining, which were invaluable in bringing us closer together. Between meetings, I tried to communicate better through monthly email updates, and soon did away with our board calls unless there was an important issue to discuss. While I never entirely lost the anxiety and stress that came with preparing for a meeting, our board became very valuable to me, and was instrumental in the success we later experienced.

I also tried, from time to time, to have some fun. On April 1, 2014 I emailed the board a convincing update on a humanitarian relief e-voucher payment project we had contracted following the Ukrainian Revolution. I explained that we were sending an advance team to set up an office in Kiev and would be halting all of the priorities we had agreed on at the last board meeting because of the need and opportunity in Ukraine. Charles called me later that night to tell me he had needed to take a long walk after reading my update because he was so angry that we were ignoring his advice to stop chasing distractions and focus. Then he remembered what day it was.

EMBRACING FAILURE: WHAT I LEARNED

Managing a board is a critical part of a venture-backed startup CEO's job. This in itself is a key understanding. It is also a major source of stress and anxiety that can become all-encompassing. If I could do it over again, I would push to start off with the smallest possible board and the lightest possible formal governance processes. This was challenging given our founding team structure, but we could have been creative and established a three- or maximum five-person board, alongside a network of external advisors outside of our governance net. For a long time, we simply had too many people in the room and prioritized process over content. Besides, we never once had a board vote that wasn't unanimous, so any up-front concerns of balancing founder versus investor control were largely unfounded. Moreover, they were sufficiently dealt with by shareholder level protections that guarded against the board taking unilateral or reckless actions.

I learned over time that the value of the board is generated from strong relationships, so I would maintain the practice of mandatory board dinners (before meetings) and general time together outside of meetings. This is where the conversations really take off and new sparks are generated. If the board is remote and scattered, virtual meetings can be effective — and are much more cost- and time-efficient — but a full or multi-day board retreat once or twice a year will bring everyone into alignment and create a lot of value that pays off later.

Preparing for board meetings takes a lot of work, so I would streamline the admin as much as possible by scheduling meetings well in advance, with no date or location changes permitted unless absolutely necessary. I would keep board packs lean, with one master slide deck to frame discussion questions, and only include relevant supporting materials.

There should be a clear expectation that the materials are read in advance, with questions from board members pre-circulated to the CEO to ensure that this is indeed the case, and to help the CEO prepare and save time during the meeting. The actual meeting agenda should be designed for generative discussion, not reporting, updating or pushing opinionated individual agendas. Everyone should be expected to show up wearing the right hat, and the CEO or chair should start each meeting with this reminder.

Finally, I would set the tone that the principal responsibility of the board is to give value to the CEO and the founding team, not extract it. Founders need to do their part to create the space for this to happen and lean into external insights and wisdom, even when they are uncomfortable. Once this becomes a shared norm, the board will gradually grow in value and become more than a governance or oversight filter; it will become a genuine strategic asset to the company.

CHAPTER 5
FAILING TO FOCUS

When we closed our Series A, none of us — neither founders nor investors — really believed that our over-the-counter money transfer product would take us to the promised land. Brad and Brett had always been dead-set against building a consumer brand, which they were sure would eventually get crushed by M-Pesa mobile money copycat products from the large, deep-pocketed mobile network operators (MNOs). Money transfers were a short-term strategy to generate revenue and build up a cash-in and cash-out agent network that we could leverage for a more defensible business-to-business (B2B) opportunity: Offering one-to-many and many-to-one "enterprise" payment services to large organizations that needed to transact with unbanked consumers.

We were, however, first-to-market in Zambia with consumer money transfers, and the exponential success of M-Pesa in Kenya was hard to ignore. What if we could scale up quickly and capture the consumer market before the MNOs woke up? Could we become the "M-Pesa of Zambia"?

This tug-of-war between two strategies based on opposing assumptions became the fundamental dilemma of the company, and perhaps the foundation of many of the problems we were to encounter in the years ahead. We were always able to rationalize any new opportunity as part of our overarching strategy, and lacked both the wisdom and discipline to prioritize and sequence properly. In this pursuit of doing everything, we failed to focus on the core that was driving our growth, margin and impact. In fact, it took us a long time and a lot of failing to even figure out what our core was.

E-Vouchers

Zoona originally came into being on the back of a catalyzing seed grant in 2007 from PROFIT, a USAID-funded NGO. Then in 2009, just as we were launching our champion agent model, Brad and Brett rekindled their relationship with PROFIT to design an electronic voucher product (e-vouchers, for short) that would enable donors and NGOs to distribute smart subsidies to targeted beneficiaries. An NGO client could pre-register beneficiaries on our system and provide them with single-use physical scratch cards, which eliminated the need for a bearer to own a mobile phone or memorize a personal identification number that could be easily forgotten. Once presented to a pre-registered retailer, our system would validate the scratch card reference number against the beneficiary's ID number to ensure they matched, and confirm that the subsidy was still valid. If approved, the retailer would receive an instant electronic payment from the NGO and could then hand over the goods, with redemption data feeding into a real-time dashboard that the NGO could monitor.

PROFIT loved the e-voucher system design. They paid for the technology development with a grant and found a local agricultural NGO to pilot it to distribute seed and fertilizer subsidies to smallholder farmers. The pilot project led to Brad and Brett being introduced to the Zambia office of the

United Nations World Food Programme (WFP), which was looking for a better way to deliver nutritious monthly food baskets to thousands of HIV/AIDS beneficiaries. Previously, these beneficiaries had to stand in long queues, which publicly revealed their HIV-positive status, to receive food that the WFP procured and distributed themselves. With our e-voucher system, beneficiaries could redeem scratch cards discreetly at their community grocery stores, where they would be treated as regular paying customers. All of the procurement and distribution would shift from the WFP to private sector retailers, saving donor money and benefiting the local economy.

The WFP bit immediately and signed a pilot contract. Even before we had completed a real transaction, they insisted on a high-profile launch ceremony with national press coverage and a live demonstration for a government minister. Despite a last-second systems glitch, Brad pulled off the demo, and before long we were redeeming 30,000 e-vouchers per month. Encouraged by the traction, we started working with the WFP to expand the project into new markets. We licensed the technology to their Zimbabwe and Mozambique entities and even set up a joint venture in Zimbabwe called Redan Mobile Transactions, in partnership with Redan Petroleum, a prominent fuel company that had a network of retail stores.

After WFP Zambia canceled their contract and left us high and dry following the sudden shift in their funding priorities in late 2010 (as described in chapter 2), the Zimbabwe and Mozambique projects continued to limp along at much smaller volumes. Meanwhile, the WFP's sister organization, the Food and Agriculture Organization (FAO), contracted us to distribute e-vouchers for fertilizer subsidies to thousands of smallholder farmers. The FAO project was intended as a proof of concept to pitch the Zambian government to adopt e-vouchers for its huge Fertilizer Input Support Programme, which distributed paper vouchers to a million maize farmers every year. These paper vouchers had a way of ending up in the wrong hands, and the donor countries that contributed millions of dollars in funding were calling for transparency. We believed our e-voucher system provided the solution.

Every agricultural season, we would invest time and money in upgrading our e-voucher system in anticipation of a promised government tender. For several years, the tenders never materialized, and when they finally did — often with very little notice and too late in the agricultural season — we would do the work to submit a proposal, but either the tender would be canceled or we wouldn't be selected. Ironically, even though our efforts were focused on Zambia, we ended up winning a tender one year to pilot fertilizer e-vouchers with the government of Malawi. The pilot was successful but the project wasn't scaled up. It seemed that vested interests, politics and funding were the real decision-making drivers, and despite our best efforts e-vouchers never took off.

Bulk Payments

We had learned from our early experience building the system to pay Dunavant's smallholder cotton farmers that there was enormous demand for one-to-many bulk payments from corporates to unbanked recipients. It proved to be too difficult to establish a rural agent network that was liquid enough to cash-out seasonal bulk payments to farmers, but we suspected there was a better use case in the micro-finance sector, where micro-finance institutions (MFIs) disbursed small-value loans all year long to their clients in cities and towns.

I quickly validated this theory after visiting the Lusaka head office of an MFI called Vision Fund, where I counted more than 40 women waiting in a small reception to receive cash loans. The CEO explained to me their constant headaches associated with managing and disbursing cash at their branches across the country, and he eagerly agreed to pilot with us. Our bulk payment product seemed simple enough: A Vision Fund finance manager would transfer funds via EFT into our client bank account, upload a spreadsheet into our system with the list of recipients, and press a button to disburse the loans. The recipients would instantly receive text messages to collect their loans at any one of our agents, who would pay out the cash in exchange for standard cash-out commissions.

The value quickly became apparent to Vision Fund, so they ramped up disbursement volumes to empty their head office and regional branches of clients. However, this created a major problem for us and our agents: Because Vision Fund disbursed loans in batches and to groups of individuals, the recipients would descend upon our agents all at once, quickly draining their cash liquidity. Those at the back of the queue who didn't get their money — or anyone who came to receive a money transfer — would leave dissatisfied, sometimes thinking the agents were purposefully withholding their funds. The first time this happened in Lusaka, one of our champion agents redirected a mob of irate Vision Fund clients to our office; I paid them out personally, using whatever cash I could scrape together on the spot from our team, processing the transactions with my personal agent account that was meant for product testing.

To keep this from happening again, we worked with Vision Fund to direct their clients to targeted agents on a pre-set disbursement schedule, to whom we manually extended thousands of dollars of electronic float on credit, which they could liquidate in advance to meet the cash demand. It took the majority of our internal resources to micromanage this process, and resulted in Keith losing both sleep and the last of his hair trying to reconcile and chase up shortages. We worked this way for nearly two years, until we belatedly came to the realization that we could neither scale nor support the project further. Vision Fund was not pleased to have their original problem pushed back to them after they had grown accustomed to the benefits of being cashless, but we were relieved to move on from an unsustainable model.

While we were rolling out with Vision Fund, Dunavant started using our bulk payment product to pay a portion of their unbanked casual laborers. During the training of their finance team, we discovered they also had a pain point paying salaries to their banked employees. There was no central banking switch in Zambia that allowed funds to move easily from one bank to another, which made it very expensive and slow for Dunavant to make payments from their corporate bank account to employees who didn't use the same bank. This ignited a lightbulb idea for Brett, who adapted our bulk payment product to also cater for one-to-many payments into any bank account, if the end recipients had one. Since we already had accounts with all the main banks filled with agent float, we could receive a lump sum EFT from Dunavant into one client bank account and then shift funds to individual recipients from whatever client bank matched where the money was heading. There was enough margin from the bank fee arbitrage for this to be attractive to us while also saving Dunavant money with each monthly payroll cycle.

Realizing this, we spotted a quick win to acquire enterprise clients, as every medium and large organization suffered the same problem. So, we hastily released a product for Dunavant to pilot, and started selling to others. What seemed like a no-brainer to us proved harder in reality; finance directors at large organizations were hesitant to trust a new startup payment company with something as sensitive as their payroll, even if they believed they could save money. It was hard to argue this point after a system bug duplicated more than $200,000 in Dunavant salary payments a few months later. We spent several painful and embarrassing weeks apologizing to Dunavant and chasing banks to recover funds from the recipient accounts, and we ended up losing $20,000 — a lot of money to us at the time — after some recipients counted their luck, withdrew the extra cash and disappeared. It was clear our bulk payment product wasn't yet ready for the real enterprise market.

Supplier Payments

During the promising growth of the WFP project, Brett quickly designed a bolt-on ordering-and-payment system to enable retailers to order stock from their suppliers and pay for it using the electronic value they collected from redeeming e-vouchers. We signed up several large commodity companies in Zambia that wanted to get a cut of the WFP value chain and were willing to try our product.

After a promising and relatively seamless start, everything ground to a halt when the WFP canceled the project and there was no longer electronic value for retailers to pay suppliers. We rushed to find a new anchor client, leading Brad and Brett to reach out to the finance director of Zambian Breweries, a subsidiary of SABMiller (now AB InBev) and the manufacturer of most of the beer and all of the Coca-Cola soft drinks in the country. After pitching our ordering system, we learned they already had a customized one and it would be too difficult to replace it. However, they were actively looking for solutions to collect payments from their small distributors scattered around the country who paid for stock in cash. We agreed on a pilot where we would register and convert these distributors from cash to electronic payments in exchange for Zambian Breweries paying us 1.5 percent of received payment value.

Converting distributors to adopt electronic payments turned out to be harder than we anticipated, as there was no real incentive for them to change their behavior, and Zambian Breweries didn't want to compel them to do so. However, we learned that most distributors were short of working capital and experienced frequent stock outs, especially during peak periods when demand spiked. Once again, we saw an opportunity and quickly developed a working capital finance product that would allocate payment credit to distributors linked to their stock purchases. The more stock they purchased from Zambian Breweries and paid on our system, the more payment credit we would give them as a positive incentive. This immediately worked.

Distributors signed up and supplier payment value increased, which in turn increased the size of our monthly invoices to Zambian Breweries. We saw a new path to scale and diverted resources to acquire distributors even faster and extend more payment credit. In fact, supplier payments for big corporates like Zambian Breweries, with the extension of embedded payment credit to their small distributors, became the main thesis for our Series A investors following their due diligence, replacing our original pitch of scaling with WFP e-vouchers. But as was often the case, our excitement was premature.

Soon Zambian Breweries started worrying about the concentration risk of a startup managing millions of dollars of monthly payment value from their core distribution channel.

This perceived risk was fueled by the recent collapse of Celpay, another B2B payment company in Zambia, which was also collecting distributor payments but not passing them on to contracted suppliers, including Zambian Breweries. Even though our payments were all processed in real time and we built an automated function to sweep electronic value into Zambian Breweries' bank account so that their funds were never held on our system, they still required us to put up a large cash deposit as guarantee. We obliged, believing that we could earn their trust with performance and scale and eventually do away with this. Unfortunately, scaling up only brought more friction and they dropped our fee from 1.5 to 0.5 percent. Suddenly, the economics didn't look as convincing for us.

Meanwhile, the rush to acquire distributors on the value proposition of cheap payment credit caught up with us. Bad debt spiked, and we discovered several sales officers colluding with distributors to steal our money. It was as if the original days of building our agent network were repeating themselves. More and more of our operational management shifted from growth to firefighting, increasing our costs without incremental revenue. We tried to persevere, believing the growth potential and investment narrative could still be true, but this turned out to be a convenient strategy for not wanting to make a difficult decision.

Defining Our Core

In mid-2014, Brad and I were invited to attend an external "scaling-up" workshop for Omidyar Network portfolio companies in Johannesburg. One of the sessions made it crystal clear to me that we had long since entered the "startup valley of death." In the early days, we saw our multiple initiatives and quick pivots as strengths, keeping all options open and trying to move with the market. But with real money now at play, the complexity of our business was increasing in every dimension and we couldn't point to anything that we were great at — or even very good at. If we kept on with this approach, it would only be a matter of time before we burnt through all of our cash and died before achieving any meaningful scale.

Once again we needed help, and once again Omidyar Network stepped up. They engaged a London-based strategy consultant, Ard Heynike, to help us figure out what business we should become. After several preparation calls with me, Ard flew to Cape Town and presented a framework to our leadership team about the importance of "scaling our core," as opposed to trying to scale several things at once. He shared several real-world contrasting examples of what happens to companies that get this right and wrong. Clearly, we wanted to get it right.

He then opened up a discussion by asking us to define Zoona's core. We quickly branched into several threads that pointed more to future potential and what we wanted our core *to be* rather than what it actually *was*. That's when Ard pointed out a simple and obvious truth that shifted all of our mindsets: 90 percent of our revenue — and all of our growth — was coming from over-the-counter consumer money transfers processed by our top champion agents, who we had enabled to open new outlets. The room went silent as this sunk in. We had spent years saying we didn't want to invest in building a consumer brand and that our money transfer product was merely a quick way of generating revenue while we focused on more strategic enterprise payment initiatives. Yet, almost in spite of ourselves, Zoona had become a consumer money transfer company with a micro-franchise distribution model. Everything else we were doing was just noise and conjecture.

With this realization, suddenly the decisions that we could never seem to make became simple. We needed to stop supporting Zambian Breweries, park any lingering bulk payment initiatives and shut down sporadic e-voucher projects. We needed to focus everyone on growing our core agent network to drive consumer money transfers. We were already winning with this strategy without focusing on it — just imagine what we could accomplish if we did!

This was a landmark moment for our team. It didn't last long, though, as reality quickly struck when we started discussing *how* to implement these changes. When we were a 20-person team with everyone working on everything, we could stop on a dime and change focus. This was no longer true now that we were a team of 90 people, many of whom had been hired to work on the very initiatives we had just decided to cut. We largely avoided the tough decisions by shifting the affected people to new tasks that we fudged as being aligned with our core. However, most employees just carried on with their existing behaviors as if nothing had changed, either waiting to be directed or not sure what to do differently. Some who didn't agree with the changes actively worked to oppose them, creating cycles of noise and internal negotiations.

The fallout from finally deciding to focus brought to the surface new problems that we would have to tackle before growth could take off. We didn't have the right team in place, and our agile startup culture was no longer agile.

EMBRACING FAILURE: WHAT I LEARNED

In the early days of any startup, it's nearly impossible to know what's actually going to work. Formulating hypotheses, experimenting quickly and implementing a plausible growth strategy are important drivers of success. The primary objectives, though, are to first discover product-market fit and then scale it by cutting out all of the surrounding noise and distractions.

In our case, this took us far too long. Once we cracked the champion agent model and consumer money transfers started growing on their own, we took this as a cue to shift focus elsewhere rather than double down on what was working. We were also blinded by our own biases, and those of our investors, toward what we all thought our strategy *should be* rather than what the market was telling us it *was*. We were lucky to be in an uncompetitive market for so long, which allowed us to survive and recover from this mistake, but we could have been so much further ahead if we had simplified our business earlier and focused all of our time, energy and resources on driving over-the-counter consumer money transfers at our champion agents.

Looking back, we also lacked the wisdom and courage to do what we should have done once we finally got there; namely, cut all of the roles that were not focused on our core, and bank the savings. This would have been the right decision to set up the business for future success, but I believed at the time that everyone deserved a chance to readjust, and that this would happen after simply announcing what our core was. Unfortunately, this proved not to be true; I was really just avoiding some short-term pain by being indecisive. As a result, we squandered a prime opportunity to get leaner and faster with a smaller team while extending our cash runway — mistakes we would pay for later.

CHAPTER 6

FAILING TO DESIGN CULTURE

At our peak, Zoona's culture was one of our strongest assets. We created a company that attracted great people with diverse backgrounds and skill sets, who cared deeply about our mission and who worked together collaboratively to solve problems for our agents and consumers. We became known as a great place to work for purpose-driven, talented people. But it wasn't always like this.

Before our Series A investment, we believed we were too small and too busy to care about our culture. The thing about culture, though, is that it exists whether you care about it or not. People will naturally default to how they have behaved in the past to determine how they should behave in the present, while also taking cues from the company's founders, their managers and their colleagues. Without any design or guidance, ad hoc behaviors — both good and bad — become entrenched as "the way of doing things"; they become the company's culture. As the team grows, the culture can morph and change with each addition to a point that it becomes critically disconnected from the ethos and beliefs on which the company was founded and the ways of working that formed the roots of previous growth. Left unchecked, culture can become a major obstacle to growth, the root cause of an unproductive, political and generally unenjoyable work environment.

We found this happening to us on several occasions. It took us a long time and a lot of failing to learn that culture needs to be designed with intent, and constantly reinforced to keep it aligned with the company's mission and objectives.

Getting It All Wrong

It didn't take long after our Series A for our culture to shift in the wrong direction and start working against us. This was largely the result of the overnight change in our cash position and the growth of our team.

At the time, Graham Lettner, the hard-working Canadian volunteer from Engineers Without Borders, was our agent manager in Zambia. He had been instrumental in establishing the champion agent model that drove our growth for years, and he had sweat with us for his efforts. In the celebratory phase after the investment closed, Graham independently informed his team members that they were all due substantial raises in line with numbers I had plugged into our investment model. There were, however, two immediate problems: First, the numbers were estimates I had made to build up a cost base for our investment use of funds, and in many cases differed materially from what people were currently paid (which was my mistake); and second, I wasn't expecting the numbers in our model to be taken literally as an indication of what everyone's salaries should shift to overnight.

Graham's premature communication to his team brought to the surface previously undiscussed assumptions that the expense lines in our budget had to be spent, and that managers had free rein over compensation for their staff. It also exposed a general expectation that *all* of our staff would receive raises now that we had money in the bank. Our founding team was not immune to this mentality. We had negotiated hard with our investors to increase our salaries, and it was only natural that those around us would learn from our behavior and imitate it. No matter how discreet we might have been, our employees speculated and ultimately found out what was going on. Moreover, it was easy for us to reason that everyone deserved a bump given how far we had come, so we generally gave in.

A step change in our salary bill coincided with an increased expectation of agent growth targets. Our model had predicted a spike in the numbers soon after the investment hit, and the four founders all demanded we pick up the pace and expand to ensure it happened, a change in tone that created tension on its own. Unsurprisingly, in retrospect, simply demanding growth didn't lead to growth, and our revenue trajectory stayed firm on its original course, upping the pressure further. At the end of 2012, Graham and his wife Thulasy (another former EWB volunteer who had also joined us to support our enterprise payment expansion) decided to return to Canada to start a family, which provided us with an opportunity for a refresh. Soon after, Lelemba moved to Lusaka as managing director for Zambia, and took charge with a burst of new agent outlets that *finally* kicked us into the next gear.

Meanwhile in Cape Town, Brett had a budget to scale up our technology team. We had no hiring process, and at the start we didn't really know what we were looking for. Brett made one important hire, a system architect (who was a cage fighter in his free time), who then hired other developers he knew. There was immediate friction between the old and new developers; they worked in different ways and displayed obvious loyalties to their respective groups. We also hired business analysts to define what got built, along with a project manager to coordinate everything. Overseeing this all as line manager for everyone was Brett, a brilliant business analyst and the brain of our transaction system — and someone who had never before written a line of code.

We had no onboarding process for any of these new hires, nor did we have a well-defined process for setting and aligning everyone on company and individual objectives or appraising performance. On arriving at our offices, fresh staff were expected simply to fit in and perform, yet over and over again this didn't happen. And at the other end of the work cycle, we lacked a process for offboarding employees, which was challenging enough anyway, given the heavy-handed labor laws in South Africa and Zambia. We soon discovered that our lack of agreed deliverables and performance appraisal documentation made it almost impossible to fire anyone. The more staff we hired, the more people problems we experienced, and the more management time and energy we burned — along with cash, of course — without coming up with any solutions, other than to define new roles and keep hiring.

It wasn't long before our Cape Town office ran out of space, so we splashed some cash on design and branding ahead of moving into a new office. It had dawned on us that none of our post-Series A hires knew about our early years; to most staff, we were a cash-flush startup with a grand vision. So we celebrated the milestone with a ceremony, unveiling poetic stories inscribed on the doors of our meeting rooms to educate all who entered — and remind ourselves — about where we had come from. This injected new energy into the business and reconnected our Cape Town team to our mission — but it also widened the growing divide between our Cape Town and Zambia teams.

The Cape Town headquarters, now firmly established as the center of gravity for planning and decision-making, was becoming increasingly top-heavy and disconnected from our agents and consumers in Zambia. Most of the Cape Town staff had never met a Zoona consumer or processed a money transfer, while our Zambian employees didn't know what our Cape Town team did, and felt like voiceless second-class citizens in our company. We were finding it increasingly difficult for people sitting in the same office on different teams to communicate with each other — so how were we expecting to get the communication right across offices in different countries, still without video calls, between people who had very different senses of each other's work, cultural backgrounds and day-to-day realities?

Outsourcing Culture to HR

To solve what I could see was a growing and increasingly complex problem, I opted for a silver-bullet solution. I hired Barbara Smith, an experienced human resources executive in Cape Town, with a reporting line to me. As was our standard hiring practice at the time, Barbara was the first candidate referred to me and the only one I interviewed. She had the right background on paper and was excited by our mission. I explained all of our challenges and set her off on her own to solve them, proud of myself for my proactive leadership.

Barbara set to work, developing an employee value proposition and staff benefits package for the Cape Town team to make us a more attractive company to work for. She formalized a recruitment process, with multiple candidates and interviews, built an onboarding process for new hires, and implemented a performance appraisal process, all borrowed from her previous corporate experience. She understood the South African labor law well and supported the offboarding of a few misfits. Finally, I thought, we had some basic HR foundations and were back on the path to creating a thriving Zoona team and culture.

Not so fast.

It didn't take long for the honeymoon phase to wear off and new tensions to arise. Brad, in particular, became increasingly agitated that our new HR processes were not addressing the real problems that he felt ran much deeper. Our Cape Town headcount, along with staff costs, continued to rise, with new recruits being better interviewed, better onboarded and better paid — yet still unable to connect with our customers in Zambia and achieve any measurable business impact. Brad started to openly challenge the status quo, arguing that we were hiring the wrong people for roles that we didn't really need, but he was met with firm resistance: We were following processes, all new roles were within our budget and they were all signed off by the hiring managers who had requested them (never mind that they were often new hires themselves). Brad wasn't convinced. He felt that we were scaling a problem rather than solving it.

The tension on our team continued to rise until Brad reached his breaking point. I came into work one morning and noticed he was fuming. He refused to explain why, saying only that it concerned Barbara, but that he respected her reporting line to me. He spent the entire day storming around stressed and upset, until eventually he cracked and unloaded on me. The next day was, it turned out, Boss's Day, a Hallmark holiday neither of us had ever heard of, which was supposedly intended for employees to recognize and thank their bosses for being such super-great people. Barbara had put together a secret plan for the Cape Town team to welcome me while swaying and singing Aloe Blacc's hit single *The Man* as I walked in the front door, based on a video she'd found of a big corporate doing as much for their beloved leader. As a cherry on top, she was asking everyone for personal contributions toward a gift for me.

I understood Brad's fury, and agreed it was a horrible idea — the last thing I would ever want was to be celebrated for "being a boss," a symbol of corporate culture that we despised but now found ourselves inexorably gravitating toward. After clashing with Barbara, Brad managed to nix the song but not the gift, and the next day I found myself presented with a nice bottle of wine and Zoona cufflinks to a round of applause. I accepted them with thanks, but reminded everyone that our real bosses were our agents and consumers in Zambia who paid all of our wages and who we existed to serve.

This incident taught me that while Barbara may have done a sound job instituting formal HR processes based on what she knew, our culture needed to be set by the founders. Brad had an obvious passion for this, so I formalized his role as chief people officer, while Barbara left to become a successful HR executive at a well-known corporate. (This was in itself an important learning: Just because someone doesn't fit one culture doesn't mean they won't thrive in another.) Brad's task was to transform us from the bloated, misaligned and slow team we had become back to the scrappy, customer-centric startup that we once were and still desired to be. This would require making some fundamental changes to both our team and our ways of working.

Girl Effect Accelerator

In May 2014, I received an unsolicited Facebook message from someone called Daniel Epstein asking for my email address so

I could be sent an invitation to something called the Girl Effect Accelerator. The message concluded with "Haha... this sounds like some type of internet scam. I promise you though, it is anything but."

It looked every bit a scam, with a long list of promised benefits and nothing asked in return. But it turned out to be a legitimate invitation for Zoona to participate in a three-week startup accelerator organized by Daniel's organization, Unreasonable Group, in partnership with the Nike Foundation. Their aim was to bring together ten emerging-markets startup companies that had the potential to lift millions of girls out of poverty.

I had been so overwhelmed with all of the demands of my job that my focus had drifted far from the impact and purpose behind the business, which was the reason I had set out to do all of this in the first place. I had lost touch with our core agent customers. Daniel's out-of-the-blue message was a good excuse to reconnect with them and do some digging to find out how they were getting on. I had a conversation with Lelemba, who told me that while men made up 60 percent of our agents in Zambia, more than 70 percent of the tellers who worked for them were young women between the ages of 18 and 25. She also pointed out that many of our best agents were women like Sandra and Misozi, and the income they earned from Zoona had turned them into the breadwinners in their families.

Convinced that our potential to impact girls at scale was real, I accepted Daniel's invitation, asking Lelemba to attend the Girl Effect Accelerator with me. We flew to San Francisco to meet the rest of our group: Two leaders each from ten startups from Africa and India, along with support teams from the organizers. We took a bus from San Francisco to a vineyard two hours north of the city. We were each assigned a partner with whom we would share a tent for two weeks; I found myself paired with a man from South India, Arunachalam Muruganantham, who had invented a groundbreaking, low-cost sanitary pad-making machine that would later be the subject of an Academy Award-winning documentary. My volunteer experience with Engineers Without Borders had prepared me well for life in a tent, and the two of us got on well, but Lelemba, who was affectionately known for both the height of her heels and size of her shoe collection, gave me an uncomfortable glare when she saw her accommodation. Nevertheless, she adapted well and also came to bond with her tent partner.

Over the next two weeks, we spent time with dozens of expert mentors, including bestselling marketing author Seth Godin and highly successful entrepreneur Jeff Hoffman. As a personal highlight for me, Patrick Pichette and his wife graciously made the journey up from Silicon Valley to host a session with the group and have dinner with us. During the days, we had structured peer-learning and problem-solving sessions, and I was struck by how similar everyone's challenges were. At the end of the program, each CEO had the chance to present a TED-style talk in the San Francisco Palace of Fine Arts. For mine, I shared Misozi's story and her vision to build her own business empire in Zambia, along with Zoona's vision to scale across Africa.

My principal takeaway from the accelerator was clear: Zoona needed greater clarity about what we were doing and why we were doing it, and I needed to communicate this much better to all of our staff. Our *raison d'être* needed to form the anchor around which we deliberately designed our culture to *quickly* solve problems for our agents and consumers. This required more than just motivating people — it required transforming *how* we worked and *what* we did.

I left the Girl Effect Accelerator with the answers to three questions that encapsulated Zoona's vision and mission:

Why do we exist?
In Africa, people rely on extended family networks and their communities to support themselves and their businesses. Zoona exists to help these communities thrive.

What do we do?
We help people send and receive money when they need to most by providing an exceptional money transfer experience for underserved consumers.

How do we do this?
We see the untapped potential in emerging entrepreneurs, and provide them with a micro-franchise business solution to make money and serve their communities as Zoona agents.

Back in Cape Town, I presented these statements to our leadership team, and we debated what they meant to us and what changes we would need to make for them to be true. A wave of ideas emerged, and it was clear we would need to start by resetting our team.

Only A-Players
"A-players hire A-players and B-players hire C-players. If you want to build a great organization, don't tolerate anyone who is not an A-player."

This was Patrick Pichette's advice to our group at the Girl

Effect Accelerator. A-players are principally motivated by helping the organization achieve its objectives, and want to work with other exceptionally talented people. By default, they will hire people who are better than they are to fill gaps or take over where they are weak, so that the entire organization thrives. B-players are motivated by personal gain and political status in the organization and will hire less talented people, C-players, whom they think will make them look good without threatening their positions. B-players dilute talent over time, causing A-players to leave and the organization's performance to worsen.

I gave Brad, in his new role as chief people officer, the job of rooting out all of our B- and C-players, a consequence of our rapid growth and inadequate or misaligned hiring processes. At a company meeting in Cape Town, Brad immediately laid out a black-and-white approach: Anyone who didn't fit Zoona's A-player criteria was better off leaving voluntarily to save us the time and trouble of having to identify them. The message came through loud and clear and separated the company into two camps: Those who told us it was about time and those who told us it was unfair. These two camps were almost perfectly divided between the As, and the Bs and Cs.

A few people heeded Brad's warning and self-selected out with voluntary exits; for the rest we developed a lean performance management system. The design was sparked from an insight in a *Harvard Business Review* study called "Reinventing Performance Management," which suggested radically eliminating all of the admin and replacing it with a few simple questions that got to the root of how a person was delivering results and working with others. We built on this by getting a few of our best people to develop criteria about what a Zoona A-player was as a benchmark to assess their performance, along with what it meant to be a team player who lived our values in practice. We rolled this out with a quarterly cadence to show we were serious about making performance a priority, with the aggregate scores over the year linking to a company bonus pool that would only fill if we collectively overachieved on our annual budget.

We focused our performance management system on effort and behavioral attributes as opposed to deliverables. It was more valuable to us to have A-players who fitted into our team and culture and who always put forth their best efforts in service to our customers, versus lone wolves who hit their individual key performance indicators but were disruptive to others in the process. We later formalized this by adopting Google's pioneering Objectives and Key Results system (OKRs), which prioritized setting ambitious quarterly targets and counted achieving 70 percent of them as success.

It was never plain sailing when implementing these systems, but time and time again we noticed that the best people would lean into them while others would resist. Susan Phillips, our human capital advisor from Omidyar Network, who continued to coach me throughout, conveyed to me the valuable insight that creating a high-performing culture where A-players thrive requires, by definition, making the culture uncomfortable for everyone else. So, we consciously tried to encourage and enable those who aligned with us while not paying as much attention to those who didn't, nudging them to either opt out on their own or enter a performance management process. Gradually, a natural sorting occurred; the quality of our team improved, and so did our performance as a team.

Rapid Prototyping

Off the back of the Girl Effect Accelerator, we also introduced rapid prototyping, an approach I learned from one of the mentors, Tom Chi. Tom taught us how it is possible to realize 10x improvements by designing small, iterative and practical experiments to quickly test hypotheses in the real world using limited resources. For example, a traditional product development process involves a linear approach of researching, designing, building, deploying and marketing, which often takes months of internal work by teams of people before the product touches a customer. In contrast, a rapid-prototyping approach simulates micro-steps of the process with actual customers, using makeshift designs and props in place of real prototypes, collecting and incorporating feedback at every step. When the final product goes to market, usually much faster and with fewer sunk costs, it has already been iterated with feedback from customers dozens of times, dramatically increasing the probability of success.

I was certain this "learning by doing" approach could be applied in numerous ways that could help our company get faster and better. I envisioned collaborative teams identifying problems and rapid-prototyping solutions for our most pressing challenges as a normal way of working. Ideas could come from anyone at any level, overcoming what Brad called the HiPPO problem — when only the Highest Paid Person's Opinion is the one that counts. We could also use rapid prototyping to normalize the engagement of users — both internal and external — in our product and process design, ensuring that everything we developed reflected user feedback throughout.

To get started, I mandated a weekly companywide rapid-prototyping day to see how much we could learn in a single morning. Every Wednesday, we asked all staff to stop working and submit the biggest challenges they were facing. We prioritized and grouped these challenges into themes, and then assigned groups of three to five people to work on them. We encouraged people to dive into data and seek out the unexpected. We also set up "home" and "away" teams, with a team in Cape Town coordinating with a team in Zambia to run live experiments with agents and money transfer consumers. After lunch, each group came back and was given five minutes to present what they had learned. PowerPoints were banned to save time and effort and to ensure lively presentations aided by props and role play.

The first few rapid-prototyping days were messy. Some people were keen to get started while others got stuck in analysis paralysis or felt they were too busy to drop their own work to participate. Some were legitimately concerned that it might reduce our focus on previously agreed priorities (which is why it's important to prioritize rapid-prototyping challenges that are already aligned with these priorities). The key was pushing through these teething-stage problems and maintaining the weekly cadence. In short order, the process became smoother, the learnings more insightful and the feedback presentations crisper. A buzz and energy developed around the office that hadn't existed before. Hidden leaders started to emerge, unknown problems were diagnosed, and unexpected solutions started to take form, such as improved customer service scripts for our call center employees, business management dashboards for our agents, and more efficient ways of allocating float financing to agents to drive money transfer volume. Employees who were previously glued to their desks were suddenly engaging with their teammates in different areas of the business. Some of our back-office employees tested our products and talked to our agents for the first time to get real-time feedback on ideas their group had generated. Our overall knowledge of what we did and why we did it increased measurably across all areas of the business.

Touchlines

With our founding team becoming more stable and cohesive, my coaching conversations with Susan shifted, and she started sharing her vast senior marketing expertise from her many years at eBay and PayPal. She taught me that a differentiated customer experience that targets a loyal subset of core customers can win in the market against big competitors with a one-size-fits-all strategy. The key to achieving this, though, is to focus the company culture to consistently deliver on customer expectations — and over-deliver where it really matters.

Susan flew to Cape Town and we gathered our key leaders to design "touchlines," starting with our franchise agents (our new name for champion agents). We identified every sequential touchpoint we had with them, such as acquisition, training and onboarding, transacting, expanding, and getting support. We ran rapid prototypes to figure out what franchise agents expected from Zoona at each touchpoint, and then debated vigorously which of them we wanted to be known for being the best at — our brand hallmarks. Susan explained that it was unrealistic to aim to be the best at every touchpoint, so we had to make some tough trade-offs, accepting that in some areas we would be just average or even below average. As long as we were "good enough" everywhere, both agents and consumers would choose Zoona over our competitors based on the brand hallmark touchpoints that we over-delivered on.

This led us to design a "Zoona-in-a-Box" franchise agent value proposition. A new Zoona franchise agent would receive a branded Zoona kiosk, a transaction account on our platform and an allocation of float, which we branded "Zoona Cash," to ensure she never "bounced" a consumer because she was short of electronic float — our chosen first brand hallmark. (To receive cash from a consumer, an agent needed at least as much electronic funds in her Zoona account.) Franchise agents would also receive a guaranteed fixed income for up to six months to eliminate their risk while the business was ramping up; after that they would switch to a variable per-transaction commission without a cap. New agents would go through an onboarding process focused on Zoona's values and customer service expectations, and receive branded T-shirts, training and support. Once agents became profitable with one outlet, we would enable them to apply for another Zoona-in-a-Box at a new location that they identified — our chosen second brand hallmark.

With this agreed, Susan facilitated a replicated touchline process, but substituting our franchise agents for employees. We zoomed in on the A-players we wanted to attract who would go the extra mile to deliver on the agent touchlines we had just designed, especially at the brand hallmark touchpoints. This caused us to reflect on why A-players, who by definition were never short of opportunities and often already employed, would want to work for Zoona, what drove those who did to perform, and what needed to change to better enable them.

Rather than speculate, we ran a rapid prototype with several A-players on our team to learn directly from them. It was clear that they were motivated by helping franchise agents thrive so that they could create income and jobs while serving people in their communities. But Zoona A-players also loved working in a challenging startup environment, where things were often unstructured and they were constantly being stretched to figure things out and grow.

Building on these insights, we started offering travel to Zambia as a reward for our top-performing Cape Town staff, no matter their job function, to experience working for our franchise agents in their kiosks for a few days. Everyone loved this and came back with ideas of what needed to be improved and fixed. Our top-performing Zambian staff were motivated by the reverse reward of flying to Cape Town, which sparked an idea to extend this perk to our top-performing franchise agents quarterly. In addition to organizing sightseeing activities — seeing the ocean for the first time and Table Mountain were life-changing experiences for many — we hosted fireside discussions where people shared what it was *really* like to be a Zoona franchise agent, warts and all. They helped our remote Cape Town staff understand the abuse agents might receive from irate consumers who had walked miles to receive a money transfer only to discover our system was down, or the frustration they felt if their support queries were not promptly remedied. The insights that came from these sessions were priceless, and often kicked off real-time rapid-prototyping sessions to find solutions to acute pain points. It also established real connections — nobody wanted to let down our agents Paul from Kabwe or Mundiya from Mongu after meeting them and hearing their personal stories.

With a full head of steam in his new role, Brad tapped our newly appointed head of customer experience, Megan Viljoen, to design a rapid onboarding process. Within a day, they had set up several stations around our Cape Town office where different Zoona leaders would each spend 15 minutes presenting what they did and why they did it to small groups. Megan drew creative posters by hand for each station, which served as visual aids for the presenter (reinforcing our no PowerPoint rule). At one station, we set up a franchise agent kiosk and simulated a role-playing money transfer experience using real-life consumer profiles. We replicated this in Zambia, and also mandated that all visitors — including investors and auditors — go through a rapid Zoona onboarding when visiting our offices.

All of these efforts started to pay off, and Zoona's culture transformed from a bottleneck problem to one of our most prized assets. To consolidate all our efforts and establish a landmark, Brad and Megan later enshrined our top 20 "Zoona Founderisms" in a book that highlighted where we had come from and the cultural principles that mattered most to us. Our culture had come of age.

EMBRACING FAILURE: WHAT I LEARNED

When I look back on our cultural shift as we started growing our team, and subsequent reinvention, these were some of my worst and my favorite times at Zoona. I remember the pain and frustration of realizing that our culture was slipping, and the joy when it started to work again. The greatest lessons I learned were to hire only A-players, and to design culture with intent. We wasted so much time and money figuring this out, then retrofitting solutions once we did.

After we closed our Series A, we should have taken a step back, reviewed and realigned our plans, kept salary levels low and hired much more slowly, especially in Cape Town. There was intense pressure to move quickly, but it turned out that scaling up our team very quickly didn't translate into moving the business itself any faster. Rather, it created new and complex people problems that we didn't yet know how to solve, all while we burnt through our hard-earned Series A investment cash.

Instead of trying to solve our problems by adding capacity, we should have focused more on designing the behaviors and ways of working we wanted to achieve our objectives, and then patiently and gradually finding A-players who fitted into the plan. I should have recognized that culture was the responsibility of the founders, and defined Brad's role as chief people officer much sooner. In a small startup this doesn't need to be a full-time role, but getting the right people on the bus — and then in the right seats with the right behaviors — should be the responsibility of the founders. As our team grew, we needed some HR support but we didn't need an HR executive. We could have instead hired a consultant to help establish some basic HR administrative processes, or outsourced this completely.

I learned these lessons the hard way by failing, while the catalysts for the solutions we eventually found came externally.

I benefited greatly from my experience at the Girl Effect Accelerator, along with coaching from Susan Phillips and mentorship from Patrick Pichette. Having an experienced set of engaged advisors to open up new pathways is invaluable to a startup and the founding team. Most problems, even people ones, have been solved many times over by others, and finding out how is one of the important jobs of a startup CEO.

CHAPTER 7

FAILING TO EXPAND

Our vision was a cashless Africa, not just a cashless Zambia. There was never any doubt that Zambia was too small a market for our founding team and for the investors who backed us; it was a test case to build a model that could be expanded elsewhere. But after some initial success expanding into Malawi, an even smaller market, our pan-African expansion strategy and execution proved to be (mostly) disastrous, with a multi-million-dollar failure in Mozambique compounded by a failure to expand our executive team.

In hindsight, we would have been better off just skipping this process entirely and doubling down on winning in Zambia, which in turn suffered from our lack of attention. As is often the case, though, the decisions at the time were less clear and more complicated. There were several drivers that shaped our expansion strategy, including a successful market entry that gave us hope, a currency crisis in Zambia that nearly killed us, and a misguided investor incentive that didn't leave us much choice.

The Malawi Move

April 1, 2014 marked the five-year anniversary of our first money transfer in Zambia. At the time we had nearly 500,000 monthly active consumers sending and receiving $16-million worth of money transfers at more than 300 franchise agent outlets. Our monthly gross revenue was $630,000 and growing 185 percent year-on-year. What's more, we were profitable, which gave us the ability to raise non-dilutive debt capital to fuel our agent network growth. Expanding into new markets seemed to be a no-brainer — the only questions to be answered were *where* and *how*.

We answered the *where* question quickly and intuitively. Malawi, a neighboring country with a similar population to Zambia crammed into a fraction of the land area, seemed to be the lowest-hanging fruit. As one of the poorest countries in the world, Malawi wasn't a "sexy" market, but it was relatively easy to activate. Our now-experienced Zambia team could literally drive across the border to recruit and train agents, along with new employees. The Malawian and Zambian regulators knew each other well, and it was a straightforward application to get a payment license. English was a common language of business and the basis of the legal system. On top of it all, the word *Zoona* also meant "it's real" in the dominant Malawian language of Chichewa (which was the root of Zambian Nyanja), so we knew our brand would resonate.

The *how* question required more debate, but we also settled it quickly. Initially, we had been trying to figure out which products we might need to develop to *fit* the Malawi market, but instead we chose a much simpler strategy: We would launch the only product that had scaled in Zambia — over-the-counter money transfers. To quickly establish a footprint, we partnered with a well-known local supermarket chain called People's, which permitted Zoona franchise agents to trade either inside their stores behind small trolleys, or outside in the branded fiberglass kiosks that had become our trademark point-of-sale in Zambia. We also partnered with a local NGO to recruit unemployed young people as agents, with each of them given a fixed stipend and allocation of Zoona Cash float at our risk.

Our strategy worked. In the first twelve months, Zoona Malawi achieved the same money transfer volume that took us four years to achieve in Zambia, and acquired 100,000 monthly active consumers without spending a dime on consumer marketing. To show off our progress, we hosted a board meeting in the capital, Lilongwe, followed by a retreat on Lake Malawi. The questions that dominated our discussions were, "Which markets can we go to next?" and "How fast can we get there?" We had already visited Ghana, employing a consultant to scope the market, and added the closer markets of Democratic Republic of Congo (DRC) and Mozambique to our pipeline.

Conditions for a COO

This was an exciting time. After years of grunt work, we finally felt our business was poised for takeoff. Internally, though, we seemed to be constantly tripping over ourselves, burdened by far too many ad hoc systems and processes that had been built on the fly and customized for Zambia. Our founding team was great at moving quickly and firefighting, but we knew we couldn't achieve our targeted multi-country scale without the maturation of our entire operations function. We realized this would have to be an internal step-change process, but beyond that we couldn't agree on what exactly was needed to achieve it.

Brett felt that we simply needed one or two mid-level operations managers in Cape Town to clean things up. The natural reporting line would lead directly to him, as the only one who really understood our back-end systems and processes. But Brett was already overstretched, with too many direct reports. Our technology, operations and customer service teams in Cape Town reported to him, along with our shared Zambia and Malawi managing director in Lusaka. Weeks could go by without some of his direct reports getting his focused attention; adding more wasn't going to help.

My view was that we needed to hire a professional chief operating officer (COO). Not only would we gain much-needed operations-scaling experience, we would also be able to refocus Brett on product development to diversify our offering into new digital products and services. Our board also agreed that it was time for our founding team to bring in a more seasoned executive to help us scale.

We had yet to fully agree — to "align internally" — on the best approach when Brad invited Chris Miller to meet us at our Cape Town office. In his early forties, Chris was CEO of a health-tech company that had scaled into several African markets and gained a large corporate as a strategic investor. We had met him several months earlier and he had shared with us some valuable advice about partnerships. Brad thought he could once again provide us with insight into what an operations function in a multi-country business needed to look like.

After an hour with our team, Chris had articulated his diagnosis of our challenges and what he thought we needed to fix before we could properly scale. Like everyone else in our inner circle at the time, he agreed that we needed to expand geographically as quickly as possible to diversify our Zambia risk and pursue the broader pan-African opportunity before it was too late. This was a lightbulb moment for me, so I invited him to stay for lunch so the two of us could chat some more.

At the end of a long conversation that extended well past our meal, I asked Chris if he would consider exploring a potential role with us as our COO. He was taken aback, having met with us as a favor to Brad, but he was excited by our vision and the challenge of playing a key role in making it real. He also revealed that he was, coincidentally, considering an exit from his own startup now that it was becoming increasingly corporate. We agreed to keep talking.

Over the course of several weeks, Chris and I got to know each other better, and I arranged for the full board to interview him, which in turn gave Chris the opportunity to get to know the people who were backing us. Brad also invited Chris's wife for a full Zoona onboarding, which helped increase the social pressure on him to take the opportunity. I offered Chris the same salary as Brad, Brett, Keith and I were earning, along with a healthy allocation of stock options, which he negotiated hard for to offset the equity from his company that he would lose by joining us. The day he signed his contract to become our new COO was a milestone, signaling that our founding team had come of age.

Currency Crisis

As it turned out, hiring our first non-founder executive coincided exactly with our next major crisis, one that would undo much of our positive progress and permanently shift our course for the future.

On August 25, 2015, my first day back at work after a vacation, I opened my laptop and came across a news story about a stock market crash in China dubbed "Black Monday." I read the story with casual interest, then cleared out my backlog of emails before a scheduled catch-up with Keith.

Keith always monitored exchange rates because we had to manage four currencies in our business. Our revenue came in mainly in Zambian kwacha (ZMW), with a small but growing contribution in Malawian kwacha (MWK). Our Zambian entity was cash-flow positive, so we left enough cash in Zambia to cover our local expenses and pay our taxes, and then converted the rest to US dollars (USD), which we transferred to our holding company in Mauritius. The holding company then took some of those dollars and converted them into South African rand (ZAR) to pay for our Cape Town cost center.

The ZMW/USD exchange rate had worried Keith all year. It had started 2015 at 6.4 and gradually fell to 7.7 by the beginning of August, effectively negating any USD gains from our growing kwacha revenue. Keith joined our meeting looking much more stressed than I was, and told me how the kwacha had depreciated sharply to 8.2 that morning. It turned out the stock market turbulence in China was having a knock-on effect on copper prices, because China was a huge consumer of copper. With Zambia's economy highly dependent on copper production, the Zambian kwacha was crashing.

We quickly modeled a worst-case scenario, with the ZMW/USD exchange rate depreciating to 10 by the end of the year, and concluded that we could manage our cash flow as long as we didn't make any new hires. I immediately gathered our managers and team leaders and delivered the disappointing news: We had to prepare for a downside currency scenario and change our plans accordingly.

The following Monday, we held a company-wide quarterly planning meeting. I gave a presentation first thing in the morning, again highlighting our need to be prudent. It was prescient. By the end of the day, the exchange rate stood at 8.8; by the end of the week it had broken 10, already matching our worst-case model. The situation had escalated into a crisis. We adjusted our model for a new ZMW/USD scenario of 12 and realized that this would put us in default of senior debt covenants we had with two lenders, who could then technically call for their money back. This would bankrupt us. To make matters worse, it would also mean that we couldn't call on a contracted $1-million debt tranche from a lender we were counting on in our forecasted cash flow.

I sent an update with an action plan to our board, and we immediately executed a round of layoffs and cost-cutting measures. Keith updated our lenders, who were very supportive. They gave us covenant waivers to ensure they didn't call on their loans, but confirmed the $1-million tranche wouldn't be forthcoming. To fill this gap, I canvassed Arjuna and Monica for bridge financing. Both were empathetic and sprang into action, promising to go to their Omidyar Network and Accion investment committees, while also initiating conversations to request participation in a bridge round from Sarona and our newest shareholder, the Lundin Foundation, which had purchased a small equity stake.

Although our investors were moving with great speed, the crisis was escalating faster. By Friday, September 25, a month after the China crash, the Zambian kwacha had depreciated to 10.7. The following Monday it was at 11.9. The next Friday it hit 12.4. It had depreciated by 61 percent in just two months and 94 percent since the beginning of the year, with no sign of the situation improving. The major copper mines in Zambia announced mass layoffs, triggering critical ripple effects across the economy, and inflation jumped to an all-time high of 6.2 percent *per month*.

We started to worry whether such a rapid depreciation would cause our investors to balk at putting up more cash to keep us afloat, even if they had the best of intentions. It would take months for the changes in our cost base to have an impact, and the extreme hit to our USD revenue meant that we wouldn't have enough cash to make payroll beyond the next month. Stress levels spiked as we feared that everything we had built was in danger of being swept away.

Series B

Despite the currency crisis, our business fundamentals were still very strong. Even as the crisis accelerated throughout August and September, we set records by acquiring 85,000 first-time money transfer consumers in each of those months. People still needed to send and receive money, perhaps more than ever given the surging unemployment and inflation.

I had lunch with Justin Stanford, our Cape Town-based independent director, who suggested that it might be a good time, perhaps counterintuitively, to raise a Series B equity round. We had been consistently profitable for two years and, as a result, had been planning to expand on our retained earnings leveraged with non-dilutive debt financing, but the currency crisis had now flipped this calculus. We had just acquired first-hand experience of the type of macroeconomic shock that we always knew was probable in Africa, and we needed a much bigger cash cushion to weather any more shocks that might come our way. A new injection of equity could enable faster expansion into new markets to mitigate the concentration risk we faced in Zambia, and our early success in Malawi was proof of concept that our franchise agent and over-the-counter money transfer model could be exported. We could position Zoona as a diamond in the rough, a great opportunity for an investor sniffing for African expansion opportunities.

I organized a board call to propose the Series B idea, and everyone agreed it made good sense. Ironically, declaring our intent to raise another equity round also made it easier for our shareholders to get us the bridge financing we needed, because it would offer their investment committees comfort that a bigger equity investment was on the horizon. Just days later, Monica called to give me the welcome news that Zoona's shareholders had agreed to advance us $2-million toward the round, even though we had only asked for half that amount. Everyone was still bullish on the business and wanted us to have enough buffer to survive the currency crisis while continuing to execute on our plan. It was a reminder that we had chosen our investors well; all that foundational effort put into building relationships with our board had paid off.

The Zambian kwacha went on to bottom out at 14 in mid-November, an 82 percent decrease from the start of August and 119 percent decrease from the start of the year. The Zambian central bank finally intervened by hiking interest rates and actively buying kwacha in the currency markets using borrowed funds from eurobonds they had raised. The trade-off was a worsening of the country's balance sheet, but the plan worked: The kwacha improved sharply back to 12 and then slowly strengthened to 10 over the next few months.

Severe damage had been done, but we had survived our biggest threat yet — and we went on to have a record-breaking fourth quarter.

Executive Disruptions

Despite joining us in the midst of an existential crisis, Chris's integration into our executive team started well. But the honeymoon glow wore off quickly, and it became clear that we had not fully settled on the boundaries defining his COO role. Moreover, Brad, Brett, Keith and I, over time and with external coaching, had learned to communicate almost telepathically about big decisions. In contrast, Chris was coming from the outside, with almost no time to learn what had taken us years.

I soon discovered that Chris was a strong-willed and overly confident entrepreneur who wanted to create his own blueprint for how things should work — much like Brad, Brett and me. His natural approach was that each executive should own and be accountable for his individual area of responsibility, which clashed with our established norm of collective decision-making. For example, he observed that nobody "owned revenue" at Zoona, which he viewed as a problem and one that should be his to fix. I agreed at the time to let him add revenue to his portfolio, underestimating how much conflict this would cause. We had always viewed revenue as an output of all of the input components of our business working together: Brad ensured we had a high-performing and aligned team with the right people in the right roles with the right behaviors; Brett ensured our technology platform and products delivered a competitive customer experience for our agents and consumers; and Keith ensured that we were monetizing well and getting a return on our investments. Thus, revenue was the result of a collective system. Chris saw revenue as a distinct function that he should take charge of, an approach that would create a lot of friction with our established ways of working and lead to a constant stream of frustration and disagreement.

There was also growing tension between Chris and Brett specifically. I had anticipated this, as Brett had surrendered most of his direct reports to Chris, but had a tendency to struggle with giving up control. For years, Brett had heroically designed and kept all of our operational and technology systems together, under great personal stress; in theory, he should have been liberated by Chris joining the team, but the transition to a different approach was a bumpy one.

Chris immediately beefed up our "spoke operations" in Zambia and Malawi. He implemented a system for field staff to visit agents more frequently and systematically, logging each visit into a Salesforce tracking system. This required hiring more field staff, who needed vehicles and per diems to get around. He also standardized our referral-based agent recruitment with a formal process, where prospective agents would have to apply and be screened and selected by our staff. While this all made sense at face value, adding people and processes defied our established norms — following earlier painful lessons — of trying to solve problems with a smaller team and pushing more responsibility to our agents.

Still, Chris had a lot more to offer. He introduced a number of other key changes, some of which were easily adopted while others took more time. He took a much harder line than Brett on personal accountability, which led to both turnarounds and exits of people who were either struggling or coasting. He pushed to raise prices of our fast-growing Malawi money transfers to get to profitability faster, and he restructured a few overly expensive multi-store key account agent agreements we had hastily signed in Malawi. He negotiated a commercial agreement with Mukuru, an international remittance company we had partnered with in Zambia, for our Malawi agents to pay out Mukuru remittances from South Africa. He also pushed hard against our strategy of not spending money on general consumer marketing, insisting we couldn't scale without this.

I resisted this latter push. I still didn't think we could win or differentiate with consumer marketing, and I felt our earlier decision to rather concentrate resources on our brand hallmarks of agent float and agent expansion was paying off. Our consumer marketing strategy was as simple as having well-branded franchise agents providing a consistent cash-in and cash-out money transfer experience, and as long as we continued to get that right, then the demand would follow by word of mouth. Chris disagreed, and after much debate we found the common ground that our marketing strategy would at least benefit from someone owning it full time.

I proposed that instead of recruiting another outsider, we promote Lelemba to chief marketing officer. She had been with us for four years and had already moved twice, having shifted from finance manager in Cape Town to Zambia managing director in Lusaka and then to group head of talent back in Cape Town. She commanded the respect of our Zambia and Malawi teams and agents, and also of our call center staff in Cape Town. She had participated in the Girl Effect Accelerator with me and proven herself as an effective leader, a Zambian success story, with a growing social media following and a solid network of influencers. Plus, we couldn't escape the fact that our executive team consisted of five white men.

Brad was supportive of promoting his deputy, and I assumed Lelemba would be thrilled when I told her. But I failed in the execution, revealing a bias I didn't know I had. I offered Lelemba a substantial raise from her current salary, but not enough to bring her up to match the rest of us. I reasoned that Brad, Brett, Keith and I had more responsibility as founders and more experience than she did, and that Chris was a former CEO who had left the corporate-backed startup he founded to join us, which justified his equal package (and was also a condition of his move). I pitched this as a growth opportunity for Lelemba, while she saw it as an offer to become a second among equals — giving her the title but not equal compensation.

I reached out to Monica for advice. "Why would Lelemba be less valuable to the company than Chris?" she asked. Chris had more years of experience, but Lelemba knew our business and was much closer to our agents and consumers in Zambia. And she was a Zambian role model. How we treated her would send a strong signal to everyone else.

This was an important lesson for me. I had expected Chris to negotiate hard for his compensation, but I was unprepared when Lelemba did the same. I was glad to have the chance to reflect on this inequity and fix it: I proposed a matching salary along with a fresh allocation of stock options for Lelemba, which she hadn't asked for. I also doubled down on the message that we needed to build a more inclusive and diverse team throughout the business, tasking Brad as our chief people officer with making this happen.

Enter the IFC

I was determined to make our Series B investment round far less painful and dramatic than our Series A. Our biggest challenge would be the potential for the currency crisis to spook investors, but we could demonstrate how we handled it as one of our strengths. Investors in Africa always knew currency depreciation was a risk, and they discounted valuations accordingly. In this instance, the Zambian kwacha depreciation was far more severe than any investor model would have anticipated, but the upside was that it was unlikely to depreciate further in the short to medium term. It might even strengthen, though a reasonable assumption was that it would stay flat. I could also point to the fact that our leadership team, board and investors all stepped up to help us get through the crisis. Furthermore, our Zambian growth had accelerated, which suggested that our fundamental business model was resilient to economic shocks.

By the second quarter of 2016, we were aiming to raise $15-million to expand to three new markets, justifying $5-million for each. We wanted one new lead Series B investor who would mesh well with our existing shareholders and who had deep pockets, both to fund most of the raise and to follow their money in future rounds. I prepared a pitch deck and sent it out to every targeted investor I knew or could get a warm introduction to. Keith started building an investment model and organizing a virtual data room for the anticipated due diligence (which, happily, we didn't have to create from scratch this time). We designed a process to generate interest before the end of the year, then call quickly for term sheets with a short deadline to maximize our chances of a competitive round with favorable terms.

After a round of pitches, we were most interested in the International Finance Corporation (IFC), the private investment arm of the World Bank. The IFC's brand spoke for itself; nearly every bank, regulator and government agency knew who they were (and quite possibly had received money from them at some point). They had deep pockets and were a patient investor with a long-term development focus. Their emerging markets fintech investments were led by Andi Dervishi, who was based in Washington, D.C. and was one of the most knowledgeable and connected people I knew. I had met Andi years earlier after an introduction from the Grassroots Business Fund, and was struck by a comprehensive map of the global fintech landscape on his office wall, along with his sharp questions about how we would scale up and win.

Keith and I were invited to the IFC's annual global fintech summit in Washington, which Andi hosted for CEOs and executives of the most promising emerging markets fintechs. At an IFC reception the night before the event, we were introduced to Seth Thomas, the investment officer who Andi had assigned to look at the Zoona opportunity. I went straight into pitching mode, and when we finished our conversation, Seth offered to visit our Cape Town office the following month on a preliminary due diligence trip. He came, and we took him through our newly designed rapid onboarding process and organized for all of our leaders to spend time with him. He was thoroughly impressed with our business, team and culture, and committed to keep the IFC's process moving forward in line with our timeline.

We took a few other investors through a similar procedure, then called for term sheets in early January 2016 as planned. The IFC term sheet came in first, with an offer to invest $7.5-million (50 percent of the round) at a $35-million pre-money valuation. This was lower than we were hoping for but still decent, especially given the shock to our revenue from the recent currency crisis. Our Series A post-money valuation — calculated by adding the pre-money valuation to the investment amount — was $8.5-million, so this was more than a 4x valuation jump since early 2012. We received two other offers, one slightly better and one worse, which I passed along to our board to consider.

After a round of negotiation, the IFC upped their offer to a $40-million pre-money valuation and compromised on several other terms I had pushed back on, including my proposal that we appoint an independent director to take their board seat. I wanted to build the strongest possible board that was neither founder- nor investor-controlled, but I had been cautioned by several other entrepreneurs: The IFC had a history of appointing to the boards of their portfolio companies their own employees who typically had no operating experience, rarely added value and could even be disruptive. To mitigate this risk, I asked Andi if he would join our board, but he was too busy; he instead told us to dream big and come up with the ideal independent director for Zoona to take up the IFC board seat that he could even help recruit. This was an attractive proposition and a key reason why we chose the IFC to lead our round, though it wouldn't play out quite as we'd hoped.

The Caveat

I called Seth to accept the IFC's offer, and we immediately jumped into details of the formal due diligence process to follow. Seth mentioned one important caveat: The IFC's term sheet would have to remain non-binding until the very end. This left us exposed in the downside case of the IFC not investing, but it seemed we didn't have a choice if we wanted to proceed. We had declined the other offers so that we could move forward with the IFC, so we accepted the caveat for what it was, knowing that we had to close the deal. With that, we could feel the wind in our sails again.

Keith hammered through the due diligence checklist, and — after a month's delay due to competing travel arrangements — Seth travelled to Zambia and Cape Town with two colleagues, who reported back that we had built a terrific team and business. They were concerned about our readiness to take on new markets, but after meeting our leadership team, and especially Chris, one explicitly told us she was much more confident. Their main advice was to beef up our consumer marketing activities, bolstering Chris's instincts and causing me to question my own. As such, we increased the consumer marketing budget line in our investment model, especially for the new market launches Chris was responsible for.

At the end of the trip, Seth revealed a new development: The IFC wanted to find a purely financially motivated co-investor to fund a portion of their $7.5-million, even though this wasn't specified in the term sheet we had signed. His first reason was that the IFC's investment amount needed to be on par or close to the total invested by each of Omidyar Network and Accion (including their Series A investments) so that the IFC wouldn't have disproportionally more capital at risk. He also expressed that IFC, which was a development finance institution, was concerned that our existing shareholders were too "impact-oriented," implying they wouldn't push us to maximize our valuation and everyone's eventual exit.

I pushed back hard. I had been clear from the beginning that we wanted to bring on only one new investor at this stage to minimize the disruption. I also disputed his assertion that our Series A investors were too skewed toward impact. Both Arjuna and Monica had built impressive global portfolios for Omidyar Network and Accion, and Monica had just spun out a dedicated emerging markets fintech investment firm called Quona Capital. Plus, we had Patrick Pichette in our armory; he had recently left Google and formalized his role as a Zoona board advisor. I didn't think we needed anyone other than the IFC, and we could make up for any shortcomings with a strong, independent board.

Despite my argument, Seth insisted that the deal could well be thwarted by the IFC's investment committee unless we found a compromise. Coincidentally, our independent director Justin Stanford's investment firm, 4Di Capital, was in the process of closing a new fintech fund. We knew Justin well as a respected tech entrepreneur and investor, and while 4Di didn't fit the mold of the big established commercial investor Seth had in mind, he agreed it would help by reducing the IFC's exposure.

4Di agreed to invest $1-million, and the Lundin Foundation also took up an extra $500,000 above their pro rata share, reducing the IFC's investment to $6-million.

Another sticking point was the IFC's demand for a veto right on future financing, which meant that all future investment would need IFC approval; this gave them a great deal of power over the company and other investors. Seth explained that it was a necessary requirement so that the IFC didn't end up as a shareholder in a company that went on to violate the IFC's stringent environmental, social and governance policies. Despite my objections, it again seemed we didn't have much of a choice. I was comforted, at least, by Seth's assurance that, in his experience, the IFC *always* participated its pro rata share in follow-on investment rounds. He couldn't, however, agree to enshrine this principle in our legal documents — an omission that would turn out to have dire consequences for us.

After several more weeks of back-and-forth, the IFC team finally presented to their investment committee in early May 2016. I was confident, given the compromises we had made. Our business was also continuing to grow and had started to recover from the currency crisis, with our Zambia revenue back to more than $1-million per month. It seemed a foregone conclusion that the investment would be approved and we would be full steam ahead. Even Brad, who was always anxious when awaiting investor news, was calm.

When Seth finally called me after the meeting, he gave me the disconcerting news that the IFC investment committee had *not* approved the investment — but he was quick to add that they hadn't said no either. He explained that they were nervous about continued currency risk, and now wanted to tie their investment to our geographic expansion plans to diversify our Zambia exposure. This meant that for the deal to be approved, the IFC would need to split their investment into two tranches, with the second tranche disbursed the following April conditional on achieving revenue and expansion milestones. The IFC also wanted the right to independently demand an exit for their shares after a period of time, irrespective of the company's or other shareholders' plans.

I wasn't happy about this. I felt we had already negotiated the key terms in our term sheet and had made material compromises over the course of the due diligence. I made it clear that we wanted the investment in a single tranche, having turned down two other single tranche offers, including one at a higher valuation. Seth explained that these were non-negotiable conditions from his investment committee and that his hands were tied.

I circled back to Keith and we proposed a revenue milestone that was 30 percent below the plan we had built, which we were confident we could achieve as long as the Zambian kwacha didn't dive significantly again. I also chatted to Chris, whose market expansion plan targeted 500 new agent outlets by March 2017; I also reduced this by 30 percent and proposed 350 outlets. Seth accepted both proposals and we also agreed on the IFC having a right to initiate an exit process for their shares without guarantee of a successful outcome after eight years. As token compensation for the last-minute change in terms, the IFC agreed to invest the second tranche at a pre-money valuation of $50-million, which was a small increase on the $47.5-million post-money valuation after the first tranche was disbursed. We signed a new term sheet and moved forward.

After a further three months of frustrating legal issues between the IFC, the company and our other shareholders, our Series B finally closed on August 12, 2016. The first tranche of $5.4-million was disbursed, calculated as $7.5-million less our $2-million advance and accrued interest. As was the case following our Series A investment, we felt more relieved than excited. The second tranche milestones were not adjusted despite the delay in closing, and we now had only seven months to set up 350 agent outlets outside of Zambia and Malawi. If we failed, the second $7.5-million tranche was at risk. With no plan B for this scenario, we got to work.

Mired in Mozambique

With the Series B money flowing in and pressure to expand, we went on a hiring spree to bring in a fresh wave of talent. Chris brought in an operations manager from his previous business, a Malawi managing director, a head of expansion and two experienced leaders to head up our customer service and credit functions. Lelemba embraced her new role by expanding her team with experienced marketing, communications and customer experience professionals. Brett, who had fully transitioned out of operations, started up an innovation unit called Z-Labs, staffed with a number of product, engineering and customer research hires. Brad did the same with his people team, hiring a new deputy and several support staff, while planning a move into a larger Cape Town office to house everyone. Even the ever-frugal Keith expanded his finance and data team to split into more specialized roles.

I caught the bug and hired a chief technology officer and a chief regulatory officer to expand our executive team to eight chiefs. The quality of talent we were able to recruit was a strong signal that our brand was growing, our employee value proposition was working and our hiring processes had dramatically improved. We also took a big step toward balancing out our gender imbalance, with women leaders now featuring in a majority of key roles, including two on our executive team. The primary goal of this expansion was to prepare for our move into Ghana, Mozambique and the DRC; in our efforts to build a pan-African company, we believed we were ready to take on all three countries at once — somewhat naively, as it turned out.

Chris initially brought some sense to our expansion plan after a closer assessment of the market in Ghana, where MTN's mobile money offering, MTN Money, was growing quickly. By his judgement, Ghana was too far away to manage the logistics of building an agent network, and we couldn't beat the established MNO. We agreed with his recommendation to drop this market and focus on the DRC and Mozambique, both of which shared a border with Zambia.

The DRC, a cash economy with 80 million mostly unbanked people, appeared to offer the most exciting business opportunity. It also seemed to be the most complex and risky. Infrastructure across the country was terrible and each region was like a country on its own. We heard horror stories about how difficult it was to do business there, with rampant corruption and constant political and economic instability. However, Finca, a U.S.-headquartered micro-finance institution, had successfully set up a network of several hundred cash-in and cash-out agents to serve their customers, and a few MNOs were gaining traction there with mobile money products. If we could figure out how to adapt our franchise agent and money transfer model to the DRC, the upside potential for both impact and commercial return was huge.

Chris sent an advance team to the capital city of Kinshasa on an initial scoping trip, which confirmed both the size of the opportunity and the complexity of the market. I joined several people from Chris's Cape Town-based expansion team on a second trip, and we had a positive meeting with Finca to discuss a partnership where Zoona would use Finca's license to build an agent network and launch a money transfer service, with future potential to serve Finca clients and even possibly take over managing their agents. On the back of this trip, Chris hired an expatriate DRC managing director in Kinshasa, who in turn took on two employees to get started. These hires would turn out to be premature. We were excited about the DRC, but subsequently learned it would take time to close a partnership agreement with Finca and obtain the necessary central bank approval before we could officially launch. In addition, there was a political crisis brewing in the country, with the constitutional term of President Joseph Kabila due to end without signs of an upcoming election. With all these challenges, we concluded there was very little chance that the DRC would contribute much to our Series B target of 350 active agent outlets outside of Zambia and Malawi before the IFC's March 2017 deadline.

We were therefore left to focus all of our attention on Mozambique, an expansive country of 29 million people that stretches 2,300 kilometers along the Indian Ocean. Unlike the DRC, the macro-conditions looked favorable for our model. GDP growth had been consistently above 6 percent per year from 2005 to 2015, and consumer participation in financial services was shockingly low: Just 25 percent of the population in urban areas, and much lower elsewhere. Two MNOs had launched mobile money products, but they had yet to gain traction.

Mozambique's regulatory framework differed from those in Zambia and Malawi, requiring us to find a banking partner to work with. Brett had a good contact at Ecobank Mozambique, a fledgling subsidiary of a pan-African bank headquartered thousands of miles away in Togo, and had earlier negotiated a partnership to rent their local license. He then went to work to get our system ready, which also required translating our front-end user interfaces into Portuguese, the official language.

Chris took charge of the launch planning by shifting his expansion team's focus to Mozambique, setting up an office in Maputo, hiring a Mozambican managing director and team, and buying a couple of vehicles to move them around. He submitted an initial bulk order of agent kiosks to our Johannesburg supplier and rented a warehouse in Maputo to store them. Next, he directed the team to recruit agents and set up kiosks, starting with the major southern cities of Maputo and Matola, which required navigating a complex system of bureaucracy to obtain local permits. He signed on multi-store key account partners to further expand our footprint, with agreements to pay them fixed monthly fees in exchange for allowing Zoona agents to trade in their stores, a strategy that had worked in Malawi. The team on the ground also recruited and trained a crop of young agents, who were each given a fixed stipend and Zoona Cash float, which had also worked in Malawi.

All of these activities demonstrated exactly what Chris promised to bring to Zoona, and reinforced why I thought we needed a COO in the first place. Yet, despite good intentions and a lot of hard work, the results never came.

When we launched in Zambia seven years earlier with a tiny budget, non-existent brand and no processes or controls, consumers showed up to send and receive money every time we set up a new agent. Consumer growth accelerated as we got the basics right and expanded our agent network. The same was also true when we launched in Malawi, where we did very little market research, spent nothing on consumer marketing and operated with a skeleton team. In Mozambique, we had a much slicker and bigger operation from the start, with a lot of well-paid people in both Cape Town and Maputo focusing solely on a well-planned launch. Our brand looked terrific, our team was fully formed and our agents were trained, liquid and excited. But when we switched on our system, anticipating a release of pent-up demand, the consumers simply didn't show up.

This failure came at a time when we desperately needed results, dramatically increasing the stress levels on our leadership team. Chris doubled down by retreating into his corner to work harder, and in so doing built walls around him, behavior that echoed Keith's following our Series A. Not wanting to repeat that particular experience, I intervened by organizing a trip for Chris and me to travel to the U.S., to meet our investors and tour Silicon Valley for some inspiration and a chance to bond. It worked in the short term and emotions subsided.

When we returned, we hosted our first post-Series B board meeting in Maputo, where we had hoped to show off how much we had achieved in short order. Our board had undergone a reshuffle and temporary downsize with the closing of our Series B round: Charles, Justin and Donovan had stepped off, while Monica, Arjuna, Brad, Brett and I remained. Monica became our acting chair and Seth joined as an observer, with the IFC having rejected our proposed independent director candidate for their seat. This move had infuriated me; I had spent months recruiting a highly qualified candidate who had been vetted in a thorough process by our HR subcommittee. It turned out that the IFC wanted to take the lead in appointing someone they knew, which was their legal right, but in my opinion defied the spirit of our agreement and undermined both our established governance processes and my decision-making. The upshot was that we were stuck with Seth until they found who they wanted. I had a good relationship with him at that point, so I tried to make the best of it. The departure of Justin, who was no longer independent now that 4Di was an investor, meant there was one other open independent director seat, which at least didn't require the IFC's consent to fill.

The first part of a market tour went well, as we appeared to have a great team with a network of well-trained and well-branded agents. But we were missing one crucial ingredient — transacting consumers — which Seth clearly noticed. We openly discussed these challenges with the board, hypothesizing that we needed to expand our agent network to open up new money transfer corridors. We also laid out plans for consumer marketing, including the launch of a radio campaign and sending consumers free money transfers to help them discover our agents. Our board was satisfied and expressed confidence that if we kept pushing and experimenting, the results would eventually come.

After the meeting, we announced to the company that Zambia and Malawi would have to sit tight, as we were throwing all of our resources at Mozambique to reach the 350 active agent outlets target in order to release the second Series B tranche of funding. Despite a valiant effort, however, nothing we tried seemed to work. Bored of sitting in kiosks all day with no customers, agents started dipping into their Zoona Cash floats for their personal use, compounding our problems.

We ended 2016 with only 60 barely active agent outlets in Mozambique, 290 short of our target with just three months to go to the IFC's deadline. Many of these agents were only serving a handful of customers each week with promotional money transfers we had sent to them. We had practically set ourselves up for this failure: It had taken us five years to set up 350 agent outlets in Zambia, and nearly two years to do the same in Malawi. Yet we had bet $7.5-million that we could do the same thing in a few months in a market we didn't understand.

Reboot

Over the Christmas break, I couldn't stop thinking about our challenges and found it impossible to switch off or even sleep through the night. Our group headcount had grown to 205, up from 124 a year earlier, with a 90 percent year-on-year increase in monthly expenses and $600,000 monthly cash burn. Our challenges weren't confined to Mozambique; Zambia and Malawi were also struggling despite the earlier investment in operations. In Zambia, we had opened only 158 new agent outlets in 2016 compared to 407 in 2015, when we had a much smaller team. Monthly consumer acquisitions had halved. In Malawi, our partnership with Mukuru was growing but the earlier money transfer price increase to drive toward profitability had worked in reverse by flatlining growth and churning consumers.

We were aware of these challenges but were shell-shocked, seemingly unable to respond to any of them as we poured our energy into Mozambique. The tension on our team increased by the day, and everyone retreated into their corners. Chris once again dug in, putting up ever higher walls around him as he tried to fix the problems. Something needed to change.

When we all came back in early January, I welcomed our new CTO, Andre Penderis, who was blissfully unaware of our collective tension. Everyone had cooled down over the break and wanted to start the year fresh. I facilitated a workshop using the "essentialism" framework, which I borrowed from a book by the same name by Grant McKeown. To start, each person had fifteen minutes to make a list of everything they were doing before presenting to the group while I wrote them down on a flipchart. As expected the lists were long, reinforcing the notion that we were juggling too many balls. I then asked everyone to go over their list again and highlight only those items that were truly *essential* to achieving our business objectives. This was much more difficult, and led to a robust debate about which balls we could legitimately drop and how the ones that remained should be distributed.

When it came to Chris, the exercise clearly demonstrated that he was stretched too thin and was making his own situation worse by continuing to pile more onto his plate without taking anything off; he appeared to be setting himself up to fail no matter how hard and long he worked. Brad, on the other hand, had too few essential tasks, which resulted in him spending too much time looking over Chris's shoulder to tell him what was wrong, adding to the team conflict. When I pointed out this discrepancy, the two of them eventually agreed that Brad would be better suited to take over Mozambique so that Chris could focus on our challenges in Zambia and Malawi. I felt a large weight lift from my shoulders, knowing Brad would seize the initiative to change our course.

At the board meeting a few weeks later, I shared our compounding challenges openly, along with the change of leadership to get Mozambique back on track. Brad presented his plan to immediately and dramatically restructure our Mozambique operations to slim down and closely resemble how we had launched in Zambia and Malawi. He would reduce costs by laying off staff, selling vehicles and canceling fixed-cost key account agreements. He would also terminate the lease on our office and shift the remaining skeleton team to work from a small room in a building with live agent trading counters so that everyone was closer to our agents and consumers.

Our board agreed with both our diagnosis and action plan, and seemed to appreciate that we had made this shift ourselves without them having to intervene. When it came to the issue of our second Series B tranche, Arjuna and Monica quickly jumped in to say they supported changing the expansion milestone to align with the new plan, especially because we were on track to easily achieve the overall revenue milestone. Seth, who was still a board observer, was more hesitant. There was no guarantee that the IFC would agree to a change in milestones, he argued, adding that they might ask for a change of our Series B terms, such as lowering the valuation, as compensation. With support from our other investors, I once again pushed back strongly, emphasizing that it was the IFC that had created this structure very late in the process; they should take some responsibility for the perverse incentive it created to overinvest in scale before we had properly tested for product-market fit. I suggested that it would be reasonable to achieve 100 active agent outlets by March as a new target, which is realistically what it should have been from the beginning. Our expansion into Mozambique should have been a pilot, with results informing a decision as to whether to invest more to scale up. In sum, our market entry strategy had been wrong. The board agreed, and Seth promised to do his best to seek approval for the change from the IFC.

After the meeting, Brad got straight to work. He executed the restructuring and worked with the team to run daily experiments in the field with agents to try to generate demand. Communication increased dramatically and the mood changed from despair to hope that we could get Mozambique to work if we experimented rapidly enough to find a winning formula. This was Brad at his best. He loved turnaround situations and had an amazing ability to bring a wave of positive energy into a seemingly desperate situation.

Seth was successful in getting our Series B milestone changed. It took several weeks of back-and-forth and caused him some pain within the IFC bureaucracy, but we received our $7.5-million without any change of terms. The IFC provided $3-million, and the rest came pro rata from our other investors. After receiving this tranche, we were able to follow it with $3-million in unsecured debt from MicroVest, a US-based emerging markets impact lender we had been courting. We used these funds to refinance an existing $2-million of senior debt and boost us with an extra $1-million of fresh cash.

I was grateful to Seth for pushing this through. At the same time, I felt it was the least the IFC could do seeing as they had partially caused the problem in the first place. Unfortunately, the IFC were not yet done putting up roadblocks. Once they had finally come up with an independent director candidate they deemed suitable for their board seat, he failed to show up at his first meeting and then pulled out. Later, I learned that another IFC division had given a large *grant* to Vodacom Mozambique, a subsidiary of a multinational MNO, to support their competing mobile money rollout. To be fair, Seth was also annoyed by both of these things, but it was a stark reminder of the institutional baggage that the IFC brought with it as an active shareholder. By now I regretted having chosen them as our lead Series B investor; unfortunately, there was more IFC turmoil still to come.

Executive Exit

While our financial situation righted itself, at least for the time being, the situation with Chris continued to deteriorate.

Despite some honest conversations between the two of us, Chris continued to be an island on our executive team, even as he refocused his efforts on Zambia and Malawi. It was also clear that both of us were losing a lot of sleep.

By late March 2017, the stress and emotion was coming to a head, and it all exploded at a staff party when Chris and I got into a heated public argument. Keeping him on was clearly no longer tenable, and I wrote a long email to the board explaining why. I shared it with Patrick, who called to tell me he supported my decision — after pointing out my blind spot. "If you ever have to write a six-page memo about why someone is not fitting," he told me, "you're three months late making the decision." A couple of board members called me to ensure I wasn't making a rash call, but they realized I wasn't going to change my mind.

The next day, I sent Chris an email with an attached letter as I prepared to take a flight to London, explaining the need for a separation. It was a letter I would receive a fair bit of criticism for in time, both because I hadn't waited to meet Chris face to face and because I had exposed the company to risk by not engaging our HR manager about due process before sending it. But I was not due back in Cape Town for a week and Chris was out of the office on leave for another week after that. It needed to be done, and I sent it before getting on the plane knowing it would start an irreparable process. It was imperfect, but I still believe it was the right thing to do for the good of the company.

The following days were a blur. I felt sick the whole time. I attended the Skoll World Forum for Social Entrepreneurship in Oxford, where I shared some of this story at a "Fuck-Up Night" with a group of past and present Oxford MBA Skoll Scholars (known as Skollars). Verbalizing it for the first time, I realized how emotionally drained I was and how alone I felt.

I returned to Cape Town for the Easter weekend, in time to make the move into the house Isabelle and I had just bought — our first. It should have marked a milestone celebration for our family, but I kept the champagne on ice and instead wrote long emails and had calls with our investors to explain why Chris's departure was in the best interests of the company. An article about Zoona taking on the banks and MNOs made it into *The Economist*, which was huge recognition and should have been a proud moment for us — but it felt completely fake to me. It was a horrible time.

When Chris came back to the office after his leave, it was apparent that he, too, had used the time away to cool off and reflect. We had a cordial severance negotiation. I was committed to sending him off well with his head held high, while he was committed to leaving amicably. I persuaded a new investor to buy his vested shares so that he realized some cash for his time with us. We then kicked off a series of staff communications that hit the team like a bomb. Everyone knew there was a problem but they were not expecting Chris to leave.

I had wrongly assumed that with Chris's departure and our pullback from Mozambique we could quickly double down on our core again and everything would be OK. This was the right idea, but I underestimated how much change would be required just to get us back to a reset position. As a first step, we urgently needed to shrink our team and reduce overheads in non-core roles. I hastily earmarked three positions in Chris's commercial partnerships and expansion team that were no longer needed. At my peak stress, right after agreeing exit terms with Chris, I met with the three affected employees one at a time to tell them that their boss was leaving and their roles would no longer exist. They were completely blindsided. I fumbled through my explanations, attempting to justify why the decision was in the best interests of the company, and that it had nothing to do with their performance or their capabilities. I then discovered in consecutive meetings that one's wife had just lost her job, another was the family's sole breadwinner with several foster kids, and the third was four months pregnant. I didn't expect these meetings to be pleasant, but I was wholly unprepared to hear about the real-world effects of putting people out of work. My "tear off the Band-Aid" approach once again exposed my personality blind spot for thinking over feeling.

Brad and his deputy head of people, Erica Hannath, stepped in to save me from myself. After I announced Chris's departure to the company, they led these three employees through a fair exit process and explained their legal options, which included either taking a severance package or proposing a new role, which they were entitled to do under South Africa's labor law. They all took the severance package and left on good terms. Brad then announced a voluntary redundancy offer that allowed several others from Chris's team to depart efficiently and respectfully without the pain I had caused when trying to do this myself.

Brad took over from Chris as COO and dove into our hub-and-spoke system between our Cape Town and Zambia and Malawi teams for setting up and managing agents. He saw much that needed to change. We had grown a large team that was following an array of new operational processes and using expensive tools for workflow management and business analytics. Despite this investment, no one could point to any data that supported a positive difference on agent performance. In fact, Brad found the exact opposite: Overall agent performance had been *negatively* affected. Our field team had been chasing targets to open new agent outlets as quickly as possible, resulting in a scattershot approach. In many cases, they were negligently setting up new outlets right next to existing ones, with some even staffed with recruited tellers who were now competing against their old bosses.

In essence, we had implemented an operational system to increase the number of agent outlets, only to dilute and upset our top-performing agents, the core of our business success, after years of investing in them. Furthermore, the quality of our new franchise agents was extremely poor; outlets were frequently closed as the owners failed to show up for work or misappropriated their Zoona Cash floats. Meanwhile, back in Cape Town, our call center was busier than ever fielding complaints from upset agents and consumers about our quality decline. Our call center staff diligently followed procedures to log tickets as part of an ever-growing backlog, but without any analysis of root causes or resolution of issues. It was an absolute mess.

Back to My Roots

I knew I had lost touch with our core business, but when I became re-awakened to both the specifics and the magnitude of our problems, I realized how disconnected I had become. The last time I'd felt on top of things was nearly two years earlier. Since then, I had been completely absorbed by one crisis after another. I was working around the clock and traveling frequently, and had four levels of staff between me and our agents, having previously left Chris to run the show while I managed our board and investors. This led to me being completely ineffective and burnt out.

During a personal coaching session, I reflected on what I could do to have the greatest possible impact on our business in a way that would also re-energize me. Thinking back to my

Engineers Without Borders volunteering roots in Ghana and Zambia, I decided to undertake a lengthy customer immersion trip. I set out to spend a full month in Zambia and Malawi, working and living with our agents and cutting myself off from any day-to-day business or meetings while I was there. Lelemba came up with the idea to document the trip and share stories, so I brought along Sevie Phiri, a Malawian from our call center who had a side hustle as a videographer.

In mid-May 2017, Sevie and I flew to Lusaka, and I spent my first day working for Misozi Mkandiwire, one of our original champion agents, in one of her outlets. In the evening, we headed back to her house to have dinner with her fiancé, who was also an agent, and she told us how Zoona had affected her life and those of the people who worked for her. For instance, a number of her young female tellers had been unable to graduate high school because they lacked money to pay the fees to be issued their exam results; by hiring them to work for her, Misozi was helping many of them to graduate and go on to earn advanced diplomas.

Over the following month, I heard a continuous stream of impact stories like this. Another Lusaka agent, Musanide, introduced me to his high-energy team of more than 40 young tellers, all of whom were thankful for the opportunity and hungry to grow into successful agents themselves. I stayed with Paul, who was affectionately known as the "King of Kabwe" for his 20 Zoona outlets, and listened to his wife telling us how hard he worked — every day except for Christmas — and how he was supporting his tellers to complete school. In Kitwe, Sandra's father explained over lunch how proud he was of his daughter, who had become one of the top entrepreneurs in the city. In Mongu, Mundiya, one of our longest-serving agents, described how he had opened new outlets in some of the most rural and isolated parts of Zambia to bring financial services to usually forgotten communities. Costa, another long-standing agent in the town of Kasama, told us with much emotion how Zoona had given him a second chance after he had suffered a fire in his retail shop. Now he had built a house and was supporting several children in his extended family as they completed school.

The stories spilled over to Malawi, where I met Elesiba, a young woman who had opened seven Zoona outlets in and around the commercial capital, Blantyre. She gave me point-by-point feedback on exactly what we should do to better support our agents. In Lilongwe, I heard a mother's initial concern that her daughter Memory had become an agent for a mysterious and unknown company — but now Memory had become the primary breadwinner for the family and had even become a landowner. When we asked Memory about her vision for the future, she didn't hesitate: "I am going to have your job one day!" she said.

While these stories were inspiring, our agents didn't hold back from giving me tough love by conveying how unhappy they were about certain things. I shared continuous feedback while Sevie filmed and produced videos that were shared within a day or two and galvanized our staff into action. Different teams mobilized to produce rapid-prototype solutions to the challenges we were uncovering. One idea that emerged was the automation of our entire agent management system, which would eliminate the need for field staff altogether. An agent could request to open a new outlet via a Facebook Messenger chatbot, which would then walk her through a series of questions to collect relevant information; once verified and approved, we would send her a new flat-packed kiosk that she could have installed herself — all at half the cost of the current system.

Now that we no longer needed a large field team, Brad proposed that we engage our Zambia employees to take over inactive kiosks and work as agents for a month at a time. Though our staff embraced the challenge reluctantly, it had the immediate effect of turning fixed-cost employees into revenue-generating agents, while reactivating a number of dormant outlets. The experiment was so successful that we followed it up with an attractive offer for our employees to voluntarily resign and formally become agents. Many took up this option, and our fixed costs dropped permanently.

In the three months after the introduction of these initiatives, our active agent network grew by 25 percent. Even better, our new and reactivated outlets dramatically outperformed those that were set up under our previous agent expansion system. Best of all, we achieved this growth with a significant, and voluntary, reduction in headcount and operating costs.

Brad and Brett continued to build on this momentum. They developed and implemented another chatbot that dramatically improved a process for agents to move money between their Zoona float accounts and their bank accounts. They also rolled out self-serve tools for frequent call center requests, such as forgotten PINs, along with an interactive voice system to automate frequent responses to queries. Our inbound call volumes decreased as our customer experience ratings increased. Now that they weren't overwhelmed, our call center staff became happier and could focus on outbound calls and customer surveys.

The rest of our team followed the lead. Lelemba and Joseph Kuvor, our head of customer experience, analyzed our money transfer pricing and recommended we drop prices immediately in Malawi, finally reversing the failed increase we had implemented a year earlier. They also recommended that we restructure our pricing bands in Zambia to make them simpler. As these initiatives were rolled out, I tapped Lelemba to lead the redesign of our agent performance management system with pro bono support from Rippleworks, a Silicon Valley-based NGO that helps scale impact-driven organizations. They assigned us two expert mentors who had a wealth of experience building performance management systems for customer service businesses.

Zambia Leadership

For a while, I had been thinking about making a key move to appoint an agent in an internal Zoona leadership role. Part of our disconnect and failings, I believed, had been because none of our leadership or staff had first-hand agent experience, which made it difficult for us to truly empathize with and work in service to our agents. So when Bob Keating, our Zambia managing director, gave us notice that he was moving back to the U.S. with his family following his wife's promotion, I jumped on the opportunity.

Misozi was a natural choice for the managing director role, given her tremendous success as an agent and her embodiment of our values. She was respected by her peers, knew our staff well and had frequently been our guinea pig for field experiments. My decision was sealed at a stakeholder engagement event where Misozi delivered a fabulous speech to Zambia's minister of finance and our board, describing the impact Zoona had had on her life and the entire Zambian community. The minister was so impressed that he canceled his next event and joined us for dinner.

Misozi was thrilled to be appointed as our Zambia managing director and was up for the challenge. I offered her an allocation of stock options for her to step away from her thriving agent business and join us as an employee, and I shared my vision for her to lead the charge creating "1,000 Misozis across Zambia." However, it soon became clear that her transition would be more complicated than we had imagined. Misozi's extended family had all become agents and tellers, and while *she* could step away feasibly enough, it was not possible for her family to do so without severe financial repercussions. This opened us up to the potential for future conflicts of interest.

As we considered this challenge, I pressed ahead and brought Misozi on board anyway. The news was well received by our agent network and our regulator at the Bank of Zambia, though there were some rumblings both internally and externally about our appointment of a "young Zambian girl" as managing director of a big business. But I was clear: If the purpose of our Zambia business was to serve our franchise agents, Misozi's years of experience would be invaluable. I was confident she could learn the rest. As it turned out, it wasn't until a year later, when she would cede the top Zambia role to Brad and report to him as our Zambia chief customer officer, that she would come into her own as a leader.

EMBRACING FAILURE: WHAT I LEARNED

One of my critical learnings from this period at Zoona is that people make or break businesses. They set the strategy, build the products and execute on the plan. People who don't fit — for whatever reason — will make the work harder and lead to an increasing proportion of time spent resolving conflict and chasing alignment. The more senior the misfit and the more heads on the team, the larger the impact. This includes investors and board members, who are also people and will have either a positive or negative net impact on the company.

In hindsight, I failed to recognize that Chris was the wrong fit as COO for our business. Brad, Brett, Keith and I had already developed our own blueprint over several years of trial by fire, and we needed someone who could implement it within the culture we had created — that wasn't Chris, and it was my fault for not working this out in the initial interviewing process. In many ways, he was too similar to us: As a startup CEO himself, he wanted to create and execute his own blueprint and lead his own team within his own culture. We all might have seen this much earlier had I not failed to fully align everyone up front on what exactly we needed the COO role for. And I compounded this error by failing to conduct a thorough search to screen several candidates, which would have given us insights into their differences as well as options to choose from. I had taken a tunnel vision approach to Chris from our very first meeting because he was the first person I met who seemed to have an answer to all of our problems.

When the warning signs became apparent, I could have addressed them more honestly and with less emotion. I could have instituted three-, six- and twelve-month onboarding check-ins to assess fit and performance, and also leveraged our board HR subcommittee for more support. The exit conversation could have been had much sooner and, for the company's benefit, before Chris's shares vested. It still would have been difficult, but it could have been more efficient.

I don't regret expanding into Mozambique, but I do regret *how* we did it. We should have treated any expansion as a pilot, executed with the leanest possible team and started with a minimum viable product. We didn't need to close a $15-million Series B and hire an oversized team, especially people in Cape Town who were required to travel, to learn that our model wasn't a fit for Mozambique. We could have figured this out for far less money and in a way that didn't harm our Zambia and Malawi businesses; the all-encompassing focus on Mozambique left us slow to diagnose the emerging problems in our core markets.

As for the IFC, it was a critical mistake to agree to an expansion milestone as part of a tranched investment structure. The IFC shouldn't have gone back on their term sheet, especially after we had negotiated away all of our leverage, but it was my mistake to agree to a milestone that was so uncertain.

When our Series B closed, we were caught up in the post-investment wave and wanted to make up for lost time. We forgot lessons we had already learned, and disregarded many of the things that were at the root of our success. Had we been more thoughtful, measured and disciplined in how we expanded our team and tested new markets, we may still have failed — but we would have been left with a lot more money in the bank, which would have been helpful for future battles that were looming in Zambia and Malawi.

I'm proud of how we recovered following a tumultuous period of failing in Mozambique and an executive exit. We were at our best driving big and fast customer-centric changes to get back on track. My customer immersion trip was one of the most valuable experiences of my life, and probably the pinnacle of my leadership. I was also proud of the decision to appoint Misozi as leader of our Zambian business, though the subsequent execution negated much of the positive intent. I should have recognized the challenges she would face and provided her with more operational support and mentoring, or made the transition more gradual to give her time to learn. Our Zambia business was also in a much more precarious state than I realized, and it would have been better for Brad to have taken over as its leader until it was back on track. We would eventually make this call, but it would come too late.

CHAPTER 8

FAILING TO LEAD THE MARKET

At some point in early 2011, Brad, Brett, Keith and I made what would become one of our best ever decisions. Standing in front of a whiteboard, we came to the conclusion that our agents should be treated as our core customers and not simply as a channel. If we could adopt this mindset and deliver on it, we believed our agents would in turn do the same for *their* customers, the consumers who were actually sending and receiving Zoona money transfers.

We had no idea how successful this strategy would be in building both a thriving and loyal agent network, with a trusted consumer brand as a by-product. The more we focused on our agents — principally by solving their liquidity challenges and enabling them to expand their outlets — the more money transfer consumers we acquired and retained. Other than branding agent kiosks, we did close to zero consumer marketing for years and resisted the temptation to launch a Zoona consumer mobile wallet (rationalizing that the market was not ready). And for years this formula worked.

It even worked when we started to get attention from the behemoth mobile network operators (MNOs), which predictably and inversely prioritized their consumer mobile money offerings over the value proposition to their cash-in and cash-out agents. For years, their formula *didn't* work; they couldn't understand why our consumer market share continued to grow despite their huge consumer marketing campaigns, larger agent networks and lower overall transaction fees to send and receive money. But their competitive moves against us were not without impact: They gradually increased the pressure on us to shift our focus and start worrying whether our consumer base was at risk unless we evolved. When we finally did, we moved too slowly, too late and with too many competing distractions. In the end, we surrendered our market-leading position, which put us in the problematic position of playing second fiddle to much bigger competitors with almost unlimited resources.

Airtel Money

When the MNOs started rolling out M-Pesa copycat mobile money in Zambia — first Zain in 2010 (using our appropriated Makwacha brand), then Airtel Money in 2011 (which had acquired Zain), and finally MTN Money in 2012 — they flopped. Each service signed up thousands of retail agents to register consumers for mobile wallets and offer cash-in and cash-out services. But their registration processes were clunky, with potential consumers required to visit MNO branches to fill out paper forms and submit copies of their IDs. Registered consumers then waited, sometimes for days, for their wallets to be activated before having to search for an active agent to cash-in. Consumers who wanted to cash-out from their mobile wallets had an even harder time finding a liquid agent who could serve them. It made for a terrible customer experience.

MTN, however, analyzed the situation differently. They saw that our agents in Zoona-branded kiosks were a lot busier than their agents working out of retail shops, even though our fees were higher than theirs; the MNOs made it free to cash-in to mobile wallets and charged cash-out fees that were less than we charged to our money transfer senders. Thus they concluded that our secret sauce must be the kiosks — and they went to war. In 2013, they planted bright-yellow kiosks right next to all of our green ones in every major town in Zambia, with the clear intent to annihilate us instantly. MTN's fiberglass kiosks, imported from South Africa, were taller and better-looking than our cheap metal ones, which we manufactured and painted locally on a shoestring budget.

We figured that if beating us was as simple as putting a kiosk next to ours, then we didn't deserve to be in business. Our over-the-counter money transfer product was simpler because it didn't require any registration documents or memorization of a secret PIN, and our franchise agents were liquid and loyal. We were anxious yet initially confident that our value proposition would hold up even against a much larger and aggressive brand-name competitor. But our confidence was shattered when I shared some pictures of the MTN attack with our board. Rather than reinforcing my message about the competitive advantages of our service, the pictures served to confirm everyone's worst fears about the vulnerability of our money transfer business. We also realized that there was a high likelihood that Airtel would swiftly follow MTN with its own rollout of kiosks, sandwiching Zoona between two deep-pocketed brand giants. To mitigate this risk, our board resolved to engage Airtel in a partnership conversation before they too attacked us.

Brad knew the new Zambia head of Airtel Money, Brenda Thole, so he reached out and pitched a Zoona-Airtel partnership.

She arranged for us to meet one of Airtel Money's most senior managers in Africa, Walingo Chiruyi, who coincidentally was visiting Lusaka from their Nairobi office to understand why Airtel Money was performing so poorly in Zambia. Walingo responded favorably and began brainstorming with us ways to migrate Zoona money transfer consumers to Airtel Money in exchange for a perpetual recurring share of transaction revenue from any consumers we gave them. Believing we had solved a problem that was their biggest pain point in every one of their markets, Walingo dangled an even bigger carrot in front of us with an opportunity to become Airtel's pan-African agent management partner. After a presentation to Airtel Zambia's chief operating officer, we had the green light to develop a commercial model and sign an MOU.

Our staff saw this move as waving the white flag on our growing Zoona consumer brand, so we worked hard to rally them around the budding partnership. We explained that Zoona's future was to become the best agent network for MNO mobile money everywhere in Africa, and it was more sustainable to align with one MNO than to compete against two. We were effectively "betting the company" on this new strategy, which created anxiety, especially since we were currently winning in Zambia. To move things forward, we mandated that everyone drop what they were working on to help make this partnership happen.

Over the next few weeks, we integrated our transaction system with the Airtel Money platform so that Zoona agents could register consumers for Airtel Money wallets and process Airtel Money cash-in and cash-out transactions on a Zoona interface. Airtel had never granted this integration to any other partners, which increased our trust in the partnership. Our brand manager, Fearne Gilson, worked with their marketing team to implement joint branding of our kiosks, which we retained as 75 percent Zoona to start. We also agreed on a major consumer marketing campaign, which Airtel would finance, to advertise and promote the partnership. In turn, we were responsible for training our agents and incentivizing them to promote Airtel Money, which we did by offering better commissions for Airtel Money transactions compared to Zoona money transfers.

On launch day, Airtel Money organized a high-profile press event at their towering head office building in Lusaka. Lelemba and Brad spoke, along with Airtel Zambia's managing director. The atmosphere was festive, complete with drinks and canapés. Wanting to counter any perception that Airtel had acquired Zoona, Fearne managed to navigate a complex bureaucratic process to obtain an aviation license permitting us to float a helium-filled Zoona blimp tethered to the top of the Airtel building. For the entire day, anyone for miles around could spot the giant Zoona blimp above the Airtel corporate office. The tactic was so effective that our call center lit up — with people asking if Zoona had bought Airtel! We later heard that Airtel Zambia's COO was not pleased.

Immediately after the launch, Walingo lived up to his expansion promise and invited Keith and me to Nairobi to present to more than a dozen African country heads of Airtel Money. He introduced us warmly, praised Zoona and listed our achievements in Zambia, stressing to everyone that we had a solution to Airtel Money's perpetual challenges of managing agents and their constant liquidity shortages. Afterwards, I flew to Uganda and Tanzania and had productive follow-up meetings with the Airtel Money heads from each country.

Despite these promising signs, the partnership on the ground in Zambia got off to a slow start. Although they were incentivized with higher commissions, our agents complained that consumers didn't like Airtel Money and wanted to continue using Zoona money transfers. Our call center fielded numerous complaints about the Airtel system going down, a problem that was beyond our control. We reasoned that these were just teething problems and kept pushing to get through them, all the while thrilled at having forged a smart partnership that would deliver revenue and momentum.

In our habitual haste to launch, however, we were still operating under the original MOU. My top priority post-launch was to convert that into a contract. Airtel agreed we could take the lead in drafting it, and we then sent it to their legal teams in Zambia and Kenya to review — at which point it seemed to fall into a black hole. I emailed, texted and called Brenda and Walingo constantly, but they stopped responding. It was frustrating, but also typical of how I knew the big MNOs operated.

Then came a press release announcing that Walingo had been promoted within Airtel and was no longer involved with Airtel Money. At the same time, the Zambia COO, Suresh Reddy, was also being shifted within the Airtel group and would be replaced by someone we didn't know. We had lost our champions in the executive ranks with the contract still in limbo — never a good turn of events, as we discovered when Brenda finally replied with legal comments on our draft contract. I was livid. All of our agreed-upon terms in the MOU had been drastically slashed. To make matters worse, the recurring revenue share from Airtel Money transactions, the most important part of the deal for us, had been eliminated. When I called Brenda to express how upset we were, there was nothing she could do. I also managed to reach Walingo, who advised that we push back, but also said he was unable to help us further given his new role.

I reached out directly to Walingo's old boss, Chidi Okpala, the Africa head of Airtel Money. Chidi had clearly not yet bought into our partnership terms, but said he wanted to see if we could find a way forward. He assigned someone else from their Nairobi team to work with me, and after another few weeks of haggling, we managed to reach an agreement on revised terms. The resulting contract wasn't nearly as good as the original MOU, but it was something we could live with. We were finally ready to close.

The following Monday morning, I woke up to several emails with pictures of red Airtel Money kiosks next to our agents in various locations across Zambia. Airtel had gone to our local supplier and paid him to make exact replicas of our kiosks, but with their branding. That was the last straw. We tore up the MOU and draft contract, and informed our agents and staff to prepare for battle. I was expecting despair, but instead felt a collective sigh of relief across the company, followed by a wave of energy. We had tried to force this partnership on our staff and agents, but they really wanted us to bet on Zoona instead. Now, for better or worse, they would get the chance to stand up and compete.

Competition Heats Up

The month after our Airtel Money partnership fell apart, a large South African grocery chain, Shoprite, launched money transfers at their 30-plus stores across Zambia for a flat fee of $1. We were now facing live threats on multiple fronts. The market, meanwhile, sent us very different signals: Our money transfers may have been under competitive attack but our numbers were terrific. Between MTN's aggressive copycat kiosk rollout in May 2013 and Shoprite's money transfer launch in March 2014, our monthly active money transfer consumers nearly tripled while our revenue more than doubled year-on-year.

We hadn't anticipated that the competition we feared would in fact become a *driver* of our growth. By creating a lot of noise, MTN and Airtel had generated a level of consumer awareness we never could have afforded, confirming to this newly aware public that we were in the lead. When consumers did try MTN and Airtel, they found themselves dealing with agents who were poorly incentivized and rarely had any float, so they quickly switched to Zoona. Plus, in our model the fee was paid by the sender (who had money), not the receiver (who didn't), which helped overcome the fact that our overall fees were higher. The more noise MTN and Airtel made, the faster we grew.

The data we collected on both agents and money transfer consumers also validated our business model. Our longer-term agents were becoming more and more profitable, while new ones were ramping up faster than ever. Consumers were sending more frequently and in larger amounts the longer they stayed with us, and new consumers were joining at a faster rate than ever.

At the time, the Shoprite competition worried us much more than MTN and Airtel Money. Shoprite stores were always packed with people and had unlimited float, and we couldn't compete with their rock-bottom pricing. In addition, consumers would typically spend a portion of the money transfers they received at Shoprite on groceries at their stores, making it a one-stop option. Shoprite gained traction quickly, with long queues for money transfers soon forming in their stores, and our agents positioned near their stores experienced sharp declines in volume.

What worked in our favor, though, was Shoprite's limited footprint. Because their service was offered in their stores, which were large and located in central areas, they had fewer and more scattered service locations than we did with our neighborhood kiosks. The market was significantly bigger than they could effectively service, and those of our agents who were positioned sufficiently far from Shoprite stores found business unaffected and actually growing. Even our agents closer to Shoprite stores gradually recovered their volumes, because people who valued their time and didn't want to wait in long queues preferred to use Zoona, even if they had to pay a premium for the better service.

Sunga Success

Despite the fact that we were thriving amid the increase in competition, we were concerned that years after launching, we still had no idea who our money transfer consumers were and why they used us. To rectify this, Brett hired Kristen Waeber, a talented American who had been working for an MNO in Tanzania in a consumer insights role. Kristen quickly segmented our consumer base into gold, silver and bronze based on three criteria: Transaction frequency, transaction value, and connectivity (how many different people a consumer sends money transfers to). She then conducted both qualitative and quantitative research on these segments. Even though money transfers were happening "over-the-counter" instead of via a consumer mobile wallet, we had the data to map out all historical transaction patterns and behaviors on a per-consumer and per-agent outlet level based on having captured consumers' names, IDs and mobile phone numbers each time they transacted. For the first time we started to get a real sense of how important Zoona money transfers were to Zambian consumers. It turned out that Zoona had become the de facto service for parents to send school fees and stipends for their children, sick people to receive money for their hospital bills, and small businesses to pay their suppliers.

After we made it through the Zambia currency crisis and expanded our executive by bringing in Chris as our COO, Brett proposed that he cut the cord from the day-to-day grind and start fresh by taking Kristen to form the new innovation team dubbed Z-Labs. Z-Labs would be a small team with their own engineering capacity to focus on developing consumer products outside of the shackles of our core structure.

I was excited to unleash Brett, who I knew would thrive in this set-up while creating space for Chris to take over core operations. He and Kristen quickly got to work and secured a grant from the UN Capital Development Fund (UNCDF), which enabled them to contract a behavior change organization to conduct human-centered design research on our target consumer segments. One insight that emerged from this research was that many consumers wanted a place to store their money safely where they wouldn't be tempted to spend it. They didn't feel that they could do this with MTN or Airtel Money because their agents were unreliable and their mobile money products incentivized spending; for example, they gave bonuses to consumers who used mobile money to purchase airtime.

We ran with this insight and rapid-prototyped a product we called Sunga, which means "keep" in the Zambian language of Nyanja. The concept was to register consumers for a Sunga "digital pocket" at a Zoona agent with a simple know-your-customer process that could be completed in less than three minutes. People could cash-in to their Sunga pocket for free, and cash-out for a fee to cover the agent cash-in and cash-out commissions, with a thin margin remaining for us. Over the long term, we reasoned, we could build up a deposit base that could be leveraged to fund a digital credit offering. To do this, we would need to partner with a regulated bank or micro-finance institution, or possibly apply for our own deposit-taking regulatory license.

Shortly after our Series B closed, Keith helped Z-Labs secure a $1-million grant earmarked for Sunga from the Mastercard Foundation in partnership with the IFC. Meanwhile, our regulator at the Bank of Zambia approved a staged rollout of Sunga as long as we stayed within the boundaries of our payments license. Among other things, this meant that we weren't allowed to pay interest or use the words "save," "account," "deposit" or "withdrawal" in any marketing materials. However, we could pay consumers marketing incentives and say "keep," "pocket," "cash-in" and "cash-out." As long as each Sunga cash-in and cash-out was matched by a corresponding debit and credit of electronic float at a Zoona agent, we were good to go.

We piloted Sunga in a single town with one of our best agents and ironed out the kinks. We learned how to find and register consumers and started to understand their behavior; for instance, how long they kept their money before cashing-out. In Cape Town, the Z-Labs team also started a "nudge unit," which experimented by sending text messages to our money transfer consumers encouraging them to try Sunga. They also nudged newly acquired Sunga consumers to keep cashing-in. After adjusting the product based on our pilot learnings, we rolled out in a second town and ran experiments to discover the best way to train and incentivize agents and their tellers to promote Sunga. We also deployed a team of commissioned brand ambassadors to directly market Sunga to consumers on the streets, because many of our agents and tellers were too busy transacting in their kiosks.

Sunga went live across Zambia in February, 2017. We registered 17,000 Sunga consumers in the first month, each with an initial deposit of at least $1, a material amount of money for many low-income Zambians. Within six months, we had registered 50,000 consumers and built up more than $800,000 in Sunga balances, and were bringing in $40,000 per month in revenue from cash-out fees, though most of that went back to our agents. Sunga went on to win a Bank of Zambia award as the most innovative new financial product that year.

The success of Sunga, which Z-Labs had largely designed and rolled out in an isolated silo, gave us a badly needed shot of energy and served as an important proof of concept for the customer-centric learning culture we had started to roll out after the Girl Effect Accelerator. Unfortunately, it was derailed by the currency crisis and our post-Series B investment challenges.

Zoona Plus

My vision of Zoona's digital future began really coming into focus when Brett and his Z-Labs team started building a new micro-services transaction platform. Brett hired a system architect named Ulvi Guliyev to design a full-stack digital banking platform from scratch that could easily be rolled out to new markets. Our legacy transaction platform, which was affectionately named "Yoda" due to its wisdom and reliability, had processed over a billion dollars' worth of transactions, but had not been designed for the scale we were envisioning.

Ulvi worked for several months to bring our new platform into the world, naming it "Tachyon" after a theoretical sub-atomic particle that travels faster than the speed of light. In doing so, he isolated himself — with Brett's support — from the rest of our engineering team, which caused many of us, myself included, to question what he was building. My unease peaked when I found out he had developed Tachyon in a functional programming language called Clojure that caused the technology experts in my network to shudder when I asked them what it was. Clojure had practical benefits, requiring dramatically fewer lines of code than traditional languages such as Java, but very few developers knew how to code with it. We were now dependent on Ulvi in a big way.

Andre Penderis, our newly hired CTO, was skeptical and highlighted this as our top technology risk when he joined. He spent his entire first week with Ulvi trying to understand what Tachyon was and how it was built. To his surprise, Andre was obliged to report that Tachyon was a work of genius and that we should bet on it. Tachyon would enable Zoona's technology to quickly evolve into a multi-product, multi-country digital banking platform with fully verified customer accounts and APIs — a set of connections that would make it easy for other systems to connect with it. We could maintain a small team and reduce our dependency on Ulvi by training other developers in Clojure. Andre volunteered to be the first.

Meanwhile, Brett interpreted the successful Sunga launch and progress of our Tachyon platform as signals to start preparing for a fully transactional mobile wallet. As we registered more Sunga consumers and accumulated more cash-in float, we reasoned, there would ultimately be demand for more than the initial use case of safekeeping people's money. Additionally, there were some early warning signs that Airtel and MTN Money were gaining traction on the back of digital airtime and bill payment transactions, which were much easier to offer through consumer mobile wallets already loaded with money than as once-off over-the-counter transactions. Zoona still dominated the higher margin money transfer market, but we no longer felt immune.

Since smartphone penetration was very low and, unlike the MNOs, we couldn't build applications on our own sim cards, our only path to a mobile wallet was to access the MNO-controlled USSD channels. Unstructured Supplementary Service Data, or USSD, is a critical part of mobile communications in Africa, enabling consumers to conduct transactions on low-cost feature phones. USSD lets users dial a simple code on their phones to pull up a menu of services. We registered our preferred USSD code, *321#, with the telecommunications regulator to secure our identity, but we needed to negotiate bilateral commercial deals and integrate with each MNO to go live.

Since Airtel and MTN split the market in Zambia, we felt we needed both USSD channels to be live for a smooth customer experience, allowing any consumer with an Airtel or MTN sim card access to a Zoona wallet. We had anticipated this earlier, and Airtel had agreed without hassle. But MTN was not so accommodating; they blocked us, reasoning that we were a competitor. In response, we placed an objection with the Zambia Competition and Consumer Protection Commission, arguing that MTN was acting anti-competitively. After an investigation, the commission ruled in our favor and threatened MTN with a substantial fine if they didn't comply. MTN appealed the ruling and lost, but the drawn-out legalities ate up time. It wasn't until mid-2017 — three years after our first complaint — that MTN's Zambia CEO instructed his team to enter into a contract and offer USSD to Zoona. The delay had been costly, always offering us a convenient excuse to cut short any internal strategy conversations about whether it was time to shift from OTC transactions toward a consumer mobile wallet.

For a mobile wallet to be viable, we also needed a standard set of airtime and bill payment services which consumers had come to expect, such as pre-paid electricity. While we were battling for MTN's USSD access, we had deprioritized contracts with bill-payment merchants and missed a government tender to integrate with Zesco, the Zambian electricity parastatal. By contrast, both MTN and Airtel were able to secure contracts without having to go through a tender process. When our USSD integration with MTN finally got underway, we hastily contracted with Cellulant, a bill-payment aggregator. With this single integration and a revenue sharing agreement, we could offer all of the major airtime and bill-payment services in Zambia to our consumers.

By the fourth quarter of 2017 we *finally* had a path toward launching a mobile wallet, and we took on a product manager to lead this. To avoid clashing with the Sunga value proposition, and because our wallet was built on our new Tachyon platform, we piloted it as a standalone product simply called "Wallet." This turned out to be a mistake; it proved too confusing for our agents and consumers to have Sunga and Wallet as separate products with separate registrations. We also didn't have the internal bandwidth to promote both. When Wallet went live, uptake was limited and consumers preferred the norm of sending over-the-counter money transfers as opposed to cashing into and sending from their mobile wallets.

We needed a stronger value proposition to drive consumer adoption, which led us to look more closely at digital credit. Before we launched Sunga, we had run a pilot with Jumo, another Cape Town-based consumer lending startup, to offer over-the-counter loans to our consumers through our agents. Repayment rates were very promising, but we opted to focus our limited resources on Sunga and not extend the pilot.

We wanted to start with savings and figured we could launch credit on our own further down the line.

Several months after we parted ways with them, Jumo scaled up considerably with multiple rounds of venture capital investment, and launched a partnership with MTN to provide digital loans to MTN Money consumers in several markets, including Zambia. This proved to be the hook for mobile money adoption that we had long feared. We watched anxiously as Zoona consumers shifted to MTN Money in Zambia's Copperbelt region, where MTN's brand was strong and they were aggressively rolling out mobile money kiosks. We also learned that Jumo had surprisingly secured a non-exclusive partnership with MTN and was also talking to Airtel; it wasn't long before both big MNOs in Zambia were offering Jumo digital credit, now posing a real and immediate threat to our money transfer business.

We needed to move faster to come up with a matching offer, so we formed a team to work on it. We didn't have a regulatory license to offer consumer credit, so we struck a partnership with Finca Zambia, the same micro-finance lender we were talking to in the DRC. We worked with them to design and pilot a credit product called Boost using their license, and we went through a methodical process with our regulator to get approval. Early results were promising — especially for small businesses that required more capital than the sub-$100 micro-loans MNOs and Jumo were focusing on — but this wouldn't protect the risk of our consumers churning.

After Chris's exit as COO in May 2017, Brett and Kristen merged Z-Labs back into the core business and set to work with Andre's engineering team: Their mission was to build a roadmap to merge Sunga, Wallet and Boost on our new Tachyon platform under a common product brand and with a single registration and sign-in. After testing with consumers, we decided to drop the names Sunga, Wallet and Boost altogether and replace them with "Zoona Plus." Regardless of the mobile network they used, Zoona Plus would enable consumers to send, save and borrow on any mobile device — via USSD for basic phones and via a native Android app for smartphones (which were growing in access but still far from ubiquitous). This would be unique in Zambia and lay the foundation for an interoperable mobile wallet. A new Zoona Plus brand identity would be designed to leverage Zoona's existing brand equity while signaling that we were moving fully into digital financial services. It had taken us eight years, but it seemed that we finally had in place the building blocks of our original vision of a "cashless Africa."

The MNO Carpet-Bombing

We were encouraged by our December 2017 results, which broke nearly every record we had. We had hit one million monthly active consumers, with two million people — close to 25 percent of Zambia's adult population — having completed at least one transaction in the past quarter. We also finished the year just shy of $20-million in revenue, even with a Zambian kwacha that had halved in value since we started. These were remarkable achievements that we were incredibly proud of.

But these macro-results masked a weakening of our OTC money transfer product, which still made up more than 70 percent of our revenue. Compared to the previous year, our December money transfers had flatlined in volume and value, and decreased in revenue in both Zambia and Malawi following our lowering of prices. We could also see that low-value money transfers, which were higher margin and made up the bulk of our volume, were shifting away from Zoona toward MTN and Airtel Money, particularly in the Copperbelt Province. These trends underscored the urgency of making the transition to a digital future anchored by Zoona Plus.

Then it happened.

In early 2018, MTN once again went into full attack mode, taking on both Zoona and Airtel in Lusaka. They blanketed the city with yellow MTN Money kiosks, planting up to ten side by side on street corners. We heard stories of MTN employees being encouraged to give kiosks to their friends and family, and even become agents themselves as side hustles. It didn't take long for Airtel to respond and aggressively roll out their own mobile money kiosks in similar quantities. Within a few months, every street corner in Lusaka's central business district had one Zoona kiosk sandwiched in among a sea of MTN and Airtel kiosks; the MNOs were engaged in an all-out war for Zoona's market share.

This attack coincided with a cholera epidemic that hit Zambia at the same time. As the nation suffered, so did our transaction volumes. Following the government shutdown of markets, businesses and schools, about a third of our agent outlets were forced to close, some for up to a month. Those that stayed open served fewer consumers. Many agents took cash from their float to cover their living expenses and tellers' salaries, which many of them cut back on. Our Zoona Cash credit default rate shot up while our consumer experience degraded, with agents having less float available and unmotivated tellers. Our revenue took a material hit which again shortened our cash runway.

Following the epidemic, several city and town councils began to confiscate kiosks from Zoona, Airtel and MTN. They blamed agents as a threat to public health because they didn't have easily accessible toilet facilities. The entire economy ran on informal businesses and street vendors who also lacked immediate toilet access, but the agent kiosks were visible targets. We had to pay fines to get them back, and often the councils would relocate them to places with less foot traffic. The game of cat and mouse became an ongoing challenge, with councils raking in money through fines while scoring political points for their clean-up exercises. Our kiosks were rounded up in towns without reported cases of cholera, and each time it happened our team had to scramble to get them back.

An NGO, Financial Sector Deepening (FSD) Zambia, stepped in and spearheaded the formation of an industry association. Together, we complained to the Bank of Zambia that councils were disrupting our businesses, harming our agents, and ultimately impeding service to consumers. The discussion led to a new set of rules whereby councils agreed to standardize license fees and promised not to confiscate any agent kiosks that were paid up. Unfortunately for us, this didn't slow down the MNO attack; instead, the councils shifted to collecting fees from the MNOs directly, which meant the more kiosks they rolled out, the more revenue councils would make (which the MNOs could afford to pay). This perverse incentive enabled MTN and Airtel to roll out far more kiosks than were necessary as part of their deliberate strategy to saturate the market and take Zoona's share.

To compound the agent kiosk carpet-bombing, a regulation change that had come into effect without much fanfare now enabled the MNOs to automatically register their mobile subscriber bases for mobile money wallets. This meant that nearly every consumer in Zambia had, by default, either an Airtel or MTN Money wallet regardless of whether they had registered for one. Many had both. Gradually, our consumers discovered that instead of paying a sending fee to Zoona, they could directly cash-in for free into a receiver's Airtel or MTN mobile wallet (which many didn't even know they had). The receiver would still have to pay a cash-out fee, but this was simply netted from the money already in her wallet.

The decline of our nine-year-old money transfer product began to accelerate. All of our consumer research showed that our brand was still strong and our service was still superior, but we had lost the competitive advantage that had long justified our price premium. Consumers were fast becoming aware that our money transfer sending fees were higher than mobile money cash-out fees, and they had thousands of new MTN and Airtel Money agent kiosks to choose from — even if they had to cash-out bit by bit until they got their money. We were in trouble.

Price Reduction

Joseph Kuvor, our head of customer experience, built a new pricing model that brought us in line with the competition. We were experiencing cash-flow constraints exacerbated by the cholera crisis, so we proposed that our agents share in the pain with a reduced commission structure. Our model predicted a bump in transaction volume following the price cut, which would enable agents to return to the same income level within two months. We hastily organized a forum with our top agents, during which they all agreed we needed to reduce our fees and, after some grumbling, also accepted to share in the reduction. This turned out to be another mistake.

After some early positive signs that churned consumers were coming back to us, the predicted bump in demand failed to materialize and our money transfers continued to decline. The reduction in agent commissions had resulted in agents reducing their float, which counteracted the positive benefits of the price reduction. Worse, we discovered that some agents had been targeted by MTN and Airtel, and signed with them to hedge their bets. Since we were the only company that provided agents with Zoona Cash float on credit, which agents could easily liquidate, our float was being diverted to service MTN and Airtel consumers. Ironically, our long-time agent-liquidity competitive advantage was now driving the competition.

We were in crisis-management mode — yet again. Fearing we could lose our agent network, we rolled back agent commissions to the original level before our price change on condition that our agents hit targets and didn't divert their floats. Good behaviors would qualify agents to stay at their high commission levels, while bad behaviors would drop them to a lower tier or result in termination. It was a balance of carrot and stick, but given the aggressiveness of the MNO attack it turned out to be a Band-Aid at best. We really had to slash our money transfer prices to slow the bleeding and then aggressively launch Zoona Plus, but we didn't have the cash for the former and the latter was still a few months away.

Zoona Plus Launch

In August 2018, we finally pushed out a Zoona Plus pilot in one town in Zambia as a test before heading to the capital city of Lusaka. It was truly a breakthrough. Consumers could cash-in for free at our agents and then access a range of transaction services to send money, pay bills and buy airtime from any Android or USSD phone and on any mobile network. They could send money for free to another Zoona Plus wallet, and could optionally pay a fee for the receiver to cash-out for free at any Zoona agent. With the push of a button, consumers could shift their money into a savings account where they earned 10 percent per annum interest from our licensing partner, Finca, which was unique in the market. Consumers could also apply for a seven-, fourteen- or thirty-day loan, also from Finca, and an algorithm would instantly tell them whether they qualified and for what amount before disbursing the funds into their wallet. Everything about Zoona Plus had been designed and tested with consumers at every step, with full coordination between our Cape Town and Zambia offices. It was the best product we had ever built, and the culmination of our vision ten months earlier to merge Sunga, Wallet and Boost into an integrated digital banking product.

We made some adjustments based on key learnings from the short pilot and threw all of our weight behind the subsequent launch. One thing the pilot taught us was that consumers responded negatively to the Finca logo on Zoona Plus marketing materials, as Finca loan officers had a reputation of aggressively chasing loan defaults. This was a touchy subject because our partnership with Finca was already misaligned on several fronts, including co-branding. We made the decision to minimize their branding as much as possible for the Lusaka launch, but they had yet to commit to a subsequent country-wide roll-out.

Zoona Plus launched with a bang in Lusaka in October 2018, and the market responded swiftly. We ramped up registrations to 1,000 new Zoona Plus consumers per day following a series of consumer roadshows around Lusaka to generate hype. We converted our Sunga consumers to Zoona Plus, and our nudge unit back in Cape Town actively experimented with text messages to move them from their first to second to third cash-in, which was the metric that signaled stickiness. We started disbursing small-value loans and using repayment data to build a credit-scoring algorithm that would enable us to scale up over time. Within three months, Zoona Plus had 50,000 active consumers.

We needed to scale up nationwide to recapture our lost money transfer market share, as Zoona Plus couldn't yet be used to send money to people outside of Lusaka. Before we had a chance, disaster struck. Finca needed to approve the intended move, but instead notified us that they would be ending our partnership, leaving us without a license for the key Zoona Plus differentiators of savings and credit. This was an abrupt and unexpected shift from them just as we thought we were finally getting aligned, but ultimately Finca was not comfortable with Zoona renting *their* regulatory license for what was essentially *our* product.

All of these challenges could have been overcome if we had had the balance sheet to more aggressively slash our legacy money transfer prices without cutting agent commissions to protect our market share, while securing our own micro-finance deposit-taking license to roll out Zoona Plus across Zambia. For these actions to be feasible, we needed a big Series C investment that was meant to close months earlier by mid-2018. Unfortunately it never did.

EMBRACING FAILURE: WHAT I LEARNED

It's tempting to look back and say that Zoona was destined to be killed by the big bad MNOs. This is a convenient narrative and easy escape route to explain why we didn't win in the end; it implies that rather than venturing into head-to-head competition with Airtel and MTN by purposefully shifting toward consumer digital financial services, we should have instead leveraged our agent network to provide cash-in and cash-out services to others in the market, such as banks, enterprise clients and maybe even MNOs. However, when we did try to do this by offering enterprise payment services and partnering with Airtel Money, we found ourselves spending a lot of time and energy for very little reward.

It's undeniable that Zoona created the consumer money transfer market in Zambia, winning a quarter of the adult population as active and loyal customers despite years of competition from two MNOs and a large South African retailer. It made sense that we should not only try to retain these consumers, but expand our offering to them. Plus, our agents were dependent on commissions from Zoona money transfers for their revenue, so we had little choice.

I believe we picked a winning strategy and had a winning product with Zoona Plus, but we made the decision to move on it too late and we moved too slowly. Our critical mistake was to invest our Series B proceeds into expanding into Mozambique rather than immediately building Zoona Plus in Zambia on the back of Sunga's success. Had we taken the latter option, we would have digitally registered all of our consumers by the time the MNOs carpet-bombed the market with agent kiosks, and there would have been no reason for them to switch. Instead, we were distracted elsewhere. We also underestimated how much effort it would take to transform our team, technology, products and brand to make this leap. If we had focused *with intent* on making it earlier, I believe we would have pulled it off and become the M-Pesa of Zambia, and after that Malawi.

There is, however, a similarly critical problem with this counterfactual: It's highly unlikely that we would have been able to raise a Series B round on a strategy to win the Zambian consumer market, especially on the tail of Zambia's currency crisis. This was our dilemma: We should have focused on Zambia but we had convincing internal and external reasons not to, most notably a $7.5-million investment tranche dependent on our expansion into Mozambique. Ultimately, it was an impossible choice. Still, I wish I had recognized this trade-off at the time, and had the wisdom and courage to double down where we were winning. We could have saved market expansion for another day and with a better offering.

CHAPTER 9

FAILING TO CLOSE INVESTMENT

In August 2017, Patrick Pichette challenged me to design a breakout strategy for Zoona. "It's been eight years," he said. "It's time to go big or go home." We had battled through much adversity to reach this stage, and had finally reset our business after a tumultuous couple of years. We had learned so much through our previous failures and become a close and high-performing founding team that trusted and supported one another. The entrepreneurial fire was still burning and there was only one answer to Patrick's challenge: Go big.

At our next board meeting I presented a slide showing that our over-the-counter money transfer product had reached the top of an S-curve in Zambia with four possible scenarios for the future. Scenario A showed our money transfers being replaced by MNO mobile money, dragging our business down and implying that we should sell the business and exit while we still could. Scenario B showed a flat trajectory with stable money transfers and new value-added services that protected what we had built without taking us much further, implying the same end result as Scenario A. Scenario C showed us at the bottom of a new S-curve, and Zoona Plus's launch the following year driving a new wave of exponential growth, with its suite of digital financial services including savings and credit. Finally, Scenario D showed a step-change in our trajectory through a game-changing acquisition that once again launched us into new markets — but this time led by Zoona Plus with a pathway to becoming a full-stack digital bank.

Our board had one of its most engaging conversations ever. Everyone quickly agreed that we had earned another shot: Scenario C was the expectation and Scenario D the ambition. I was given a mandate to explore acquisition targets, which would need to be financed by a new Series C investment round.

I was excited. After the calamity of our Series B round, we had a chance for a do-over to get things right. I couldn't imagine just how close we would come — only to experience an even bigger failure when a $40-million investment round would collapse and leave our business and team on a precipice.

Series C

A few months earlier, Brian Kuwik, a senior executive from our shareholder Accion, had reached out to enquire if Zoona might be interested in buying an equity stake in Socremo, a micro-finance bank in Mozambique. Accion was a major shareholder in Socremo, a profitable bank that was virtually alone in the market as a traditional micro-finance lender to small businesses. A smaller minority shareholder was interested in selling their stake, and Brian signaled that if Zoona came in we could potentially buy out all the other shareholders except for Accion. We could then work as partners to digitize Socremo and roll out Zoona Plus, using Socremo's license to target their micro- and small-business customers. This plan aligned nicely with our Scenario D strategy, and despite our earlier failure in Mozambique, I felt that it could work.

As I started to explore the Socremo opportunity, another materialized. During our exploration of the Finca-Zoona partnership in the DRC (which was still pending central bank approval), Finca's Africa director Mike Gama-Lobo raised the possibility of Zoona merging with Finca's Africa assets. This would give us ownership of their deposit-taking micro-finance licenses, which we needed in Zambia and Malawi to offer digital savings and credit, along with their licenses and footprints in the DRC, Uganda, Tanzania and Nigeria. Our board was split on whether this opportunity was worth considering because of the legacy operations we would have to inherit, but I flew to Washington, D.C. to meet Finca's group CEO and CFO to learn more. It was clear that our visions were very much aligned, but Finca wouldn't consider an offer for any individual entities (which was our preference). The road ahead was messy, but we agreed to keep talking.

Meanwhile, I started to explore other options for securing deposit-taking licenses in Zambia and Malawi in anticipation of our upcoming Zoona Plus launch. (We were in commercial partnership discussions with Finca at this point, but there were already early warning signs that they were uneasy renting us their license for our product.) After meeting with our regulator at the Bank of Zambia, I learned that it was possible (and preferable for the central bank) for Zoona to apply for its own deposit-taking micro-finance license; this would be less onerous than a full commercial banking license, with reasonable minimum capital requirements that we would be able to afford after our Series C investment. However, there was one major obstacle: The regulations would require us to restructure the shareholding in our Zambian entity, as no single shareholder would be allowed to control more than 25 percent of the company. Zoona Zambia was wholly owned by a Mauritius holding company, which had a diversified shareholding group of our founders and investors. We saw that as passing the ownership test, but the Bank of Zambia would, idiosyncratically, consider only the direct owners of the Zambian entity itself, not the ultimate owners.

The thought of having to unwind and revise our corporate structure was an unpleasant one; it would take a lot of time and expense given we had several global institutional shareholders. There was, however, a possible way around this rule: We could float our Zambian entity on the Lusaka Stock Exchange (LUSE) and offer 25 percent of the shares to the public. An initial public offering (IPO) of our Zambian company would not only enable us to apply for the regulatory license we needed to offer savings and credit, it would also seriously enhance our profile in the market. We could position Zoona as a Zambian-owned digital bank and give our agents and consumers the opportunity to buy shares to enhance our brand reputation.

I discussed this with our Zambia independent board chair, Ceaser Siwale, who knew the IPO process well. Ceaser also gave me a lead on a distressed Zambian commercial bank that was already listed on the LUSE to consider as an acquisition target. The thought of acquiring a commercial bank was the last thing on my mind, but then I realized that this license — in contrast to a micro-finance license — would enable us to fully leverage the millions of dollars of deposits that we had sitting in commercial bank accounts for agent float and consumer (Sunga) balances. Currently we weren't even allowed to earn interest on these funds, but with a commercial banking license they could become a valuable source of cheap capital that could be used for our planned digital credit offering. The bank in our sights also had access to several lucrative government payment contracts, and because it was classified as "Zambian-owned" it required a fraction of the minimum capital compared to a foreign-owned bank. The story of Zoona rescuing a well-known local bank and digitizing it would be a very powerful one in the market.

It was energizing to have so many options, each of which came with risk but also with huge potential reward. Rather than trying to agree on which option was the best, I felt we should lay them all on the table for potential Series C investors to see who could best help us sort through them. Our lead Series C investor would have to fund the route we chose, so it would be best to get their buy-in from the start.

Everything was coming together and I was excited for the future. To help us crystalize our strategy and roadmap, Patrick Pichette flew to Zambia to spend some time with us. I arranged for leaders across our business to fly into Lusaka for an offsite meeting with Patrick, followed by a board retreat. Monica, Arjuna and Seth, who was still a board observer at the time, joined us, along with Ceaser and Shungu, our chief regulatory officer.

The meeting didn't start well. I presented all of our acute problems: Our consumer money transfer growth was stalling in Zambia; MTN had aggressively rolled out kiosks in the Copperbelt, which were eating into our market share, following their digital credit partnership with Jumo; and we were, once again, running out of cash. I shared a conservative budget we had built for 2018, which did not paint a rosy short-term picture, leading to a conversation about why we were even thinking about buying banks and initiating IPOs when our core business was under threat. This was a fair question, but I had already reached the conclusion that if we didn't do something to change the game quickly, our money transfer model was at risk of becoming irrelevant. We faced an existential crisis to our legacy business model, and we needed to be brave and act boldly.

After a break, we regrouped and started again. This time, I led with our big picture vision, strategy, strategic deal options and investor pipeline. The mood shifted positively, everyone began to see my vision and the conversation became more constructive. The board supported my call to action and agreed that we had options, but nothing was possible without an injection of capital. Spearheading a Series C investment round had become my number-one priority.

Firing Myself

Over my Christmas break, I reflected on some constructive but critical feedback that Patrick had shared with me during his visit. After nearly nine years of struggling, we really should have been further ahead. It seemed we were always "on the cusp," but had never really broken through.

Plus, our expenses were still too high. Even though we had cleared out our former operations team, we had hired in other areas of our business to gear up for our new digital strategy. Our headcount had dropped from a peak of 233 in May 2017 to 213 in December that year, yet our operating expenses were hovering around $1.4-million per month and we couldn't seem to reduce them. When factoring in capital expenditure and the Zoona Cash financing of our agents, we were still burning through more than $600,000 in cash each month.

I read a book called *Decisive* by Chip and Dan Heath, which introduced a useful construct: If I "fired myself" and then came back to work as my successor, what would I do in the first few weeks of the job?

I decided to restructure our executive team and split our business into three units. I shifted three direct reports to Brad and gave him the mandate to maximize cash generation from our legacy money transfer business. I kept Brett responsible for our digital unit, which represented the future of our business and would operate at a loss in the short term but within a fixed budget. Finally, I appointed myself as leader for our strategic business unit supported by Keith and Shungu, which included our Series C round, M&A opportunities and Zambia IPO. This structure enabled me to streamline my executive team to four direct reports while creating more accountability.

I gathered my new executive team and asked what we needed to do to rightsize our cost structure and strengthen our position to close a Series C. Brad stepped up immediately and proposed a reduction of roles through a formal restructuring process along with advancing a long-delayed money transfer price cut to stimulate demand and realign with the changing Zambian market. We redesigned our organizational chart and also decided to pull the plug on our fledgling DRC operations; we had kept this running to show as an expansion path to prospective investors but had instead learned that it was seen mostly as a risk.

These moves would leave us in a much better position a few months down the line, but drain cash in the short term. Thankfully one of our investors, Blue Haven Initiative, who had earlier given us a $1-million loan and invested in a small amount of equity, agreed to step up and lead a bridge round. To make the terms attractive, I proposed to Blue Haven's managing director, Lauren Cochran, that she invest $1-million in convertible debt to get a discount in our upcoming Series C round. Blue Haven and our board agreed, but the IFC, which had to approve the terms, felt that Blue Haven was getting too good a deal. We had to reduce the figure to $750,000 to minimize the amount of equity they would get. It was an annoying compromise, as now we had $250,000 less cash when our need was great, but it was a necessary move to close the deal.

Blue Haven's bridge investment bought us an extra two months, but we needed another $2-million to get safely to Series C. Immediately after the Blue Haven investment closed, MicroVest, who were bullish on our prospects, offered us an additional $2-million of senior debt on the same terms as the existing $3-million they had lent us earlier. This was clearly our most efficient option, so we accepted. We had the breathing space we needed, as long as our Series C closed by the end of June 2018.

Impact from LGT

When I first sent out our Series C pitch deck, several large private equity funds quickly engaged and scheduled trips to visit us for preliminary due diligence. This was a positive sign and exactly what our shareholders wanted to see. We were looking for a deep-pocketed blue-chip investor who could finance and add value to our emerging M&A strategy.

We planned to replicate our successful Series B process of hosting prospective investors in the fourth quarter of the year to learn about our business, and then calling for term sheets in January 2018 before a board meeting in early February. As the Christmas holidays approached, I was contacted by Nava Anvari, an investment associate from LGT. LGT was the largest family-owned private banking and asset management firm in the world, controlled by the royal family of Liechtenstein. The bank's impact investment arm was founded by Prince

Maximilian Nikolaus Maria himself, who had invested in a number of businesses in Africa. I told Nava we would consider them but that we had a full investor pipeline; if they were serious, they would have to move quickly and I would want to meet a partner to ensure I was engaging with a decision-maker.

Nava emailed me early in the new year to tell me their team was preparing a proposal for their investment committee. A week later, she informed me she would be coming to Cape Town with LGT's Africa partner, Shakir Merali, along with a senior expert from their London office, Marco Hunter. I started to take them more seriously and notified our board. Nevertheless, when the team from LGT arrived for due diligence a couple of weeks later, I had low expectations. I was already pushing for term sheets from other prospective investors who had visited us weeks earlier, and I reasoned that LGT was just too late. I gave them an overview on Zoona for the first hour and then ushered them into our now well-oiled investor immersion process.

Throughout the day, several Zoona leaders came to my desk and commented that they liked LGT the best of all the investors who had visited us. "LGT really gets what we're building and they ask great questions," was the general feedback. Keith and I met with them at the end of the day to discuss our investment model and process, and we quickly agreed. We didn't have to sell them on our vision and strategy because they understood it right away. It helped that Shakir was Kenyan and had experienced first-hand the rise of M-Pesa and the subsequent digital transformation of that market. He was passionate about Africa and the impact Zoona could have, and had great insights into how we could differentiate from the MNOs. His colleague from London, Marco, had a wealth of expertise in international remittances from his former job at the World Bank, as well as extensive M&A experience from his recent work at Abraaj Group, a major private equity investor in emerging markets. At the end of the meeting, they promised to move quickly to prepare an offer.

With our board meeting around the corner, I then received a cascade of bad news that shook my confidence. Four large private equity investors who had engaged deeply with us declined to send term sheets. Their feedback was all broadly the same: They couldn't get a deal past their investment committees because we were not yet profitable as a group. It was frustrating, to say the least. Zoona Zambia and Zoona Malawi were operationally profitable; what pushed us into the red were the costs we were incurring in preparation for our Zoona Plus and deposit-taking future, which the Series C would make possible. We had been operating under the assumption that we needed to make as much progress as possible on this strategy so that when the investment closed there wouldn't be a long lag between cash infusion and results. Plus, all of these funds knew months before, when they received our pitch deck and investment model, exactly when we planned on turning profitable. Either they were making excuses or they had wasted a lot of our time.

Happily, the news got better. We received two term sheets: One for a $10-million investment at a $55-million pre-money valuation and another for a $30-million investment at a $45–65-million pre-money valuation, depending on the future exit outcome. These valuations were lower than we had hoped and even equated to a possible down round, which would trigger painful anti-dilution clauses to transfer equity from founders and employees to our investors if the Series C pre-money valuation was lower than our Series B second tranche post-money valuation of $57.5-million. But they were offers from well-known investment funds and were viable options.

LGT then made an offer to invest $25-million at a pre-money valuation of $70-million. The valuation had a complex structure that took a while to understand, but once we did we were excited. If we could achieve a future exit value for LGT above a certain threshold, they would return a portion of their shares to Zoona's founders and employees. There was no cap for this incentive, meaning that the higher we could grow our valuation, the more equity they would give back to us. Furthermore, they offered to flatten the tiered investor liquidation preferences that had built up over previous rounds and set aside 10 percent of the exit proceeds for the founders and employees to ensure we would always end up with something in a downside scenario. In essence, LGT was incentivizing us to go big, but protecting the value we had already built in case we failed. Combined with a higher base valuation than the other two offers and the positive feedback from our staff during their visit, it appeared to be a terrific deal.

Our board agreed, but after our previous Series B experience, when the IFC changed terms late in the process, they advised me not to formally accept or turn down any of the offers; instead, we would multi-track them until we could make one binding. This way, we could apply pressure on everyone to improve their terms, and buy time to do our own due diligence on LGT.

I informed all three investors of our board's feedback and invited them to sweeten their offers. LGT was thrilled with the news, and signaled willingness to improve their terms and make them binding following a further due diligence trip to Zambia in a couple of weeks. The other two investors agreed to keep their offers open but didn't budge on the details. It felt like the stars were aligning with LGT.

In late February, Brad, Keith and I met the LGT team of Shakir, Marco and Nava in Lusaka. We spent a day in the market, visiting our agents, talking to consumers and meeting with our regulators at the Bank of Zambia. The next day I gave an updated presentation of our vision and strategy. The positive feeling from our previous meeting in Cape Town remained. Once again, we felt the LGT team truly understood what we were building and had many viable ideas for how they could help. We then discussed what to expect of LGT as an investor, and the team reaffirmed that they wanted to come on board as our long-term partner to help us go big. Because LGT was backed by Prince Max of Liechtenstein, they were in a unique position to be more patient than other fund investors. They reiterated that they had no interest in building a business to flip in three to five years like many other private equity investors. In fact, Shakir cited his distaste for this model as a reason he had left his job at Abraaj a few years earlier. Like us, he wanted to build something that could make a long-term impact in Africa, while being commercially sustainable.

Keith and I then met with Shakir and Marco to go over the term sheet and discuss the deal. I explained our negative experience with the IFC changing terms on us late into our Series B round, which in hindsight created an unhealthy incentive to expand too aggressively into Mozambique. I also conveyed my strong feeling that we needed to make some big moves quickly, but there was hesitation from some of our board members and investors about our M&A strategy. Shakir demonstrated his knack for creative and quick thinking, proposing a revised deal structure with LGT leading an initial $20-million round that was disbursed as a single tranche upon closing and earmarked for our core markets in Zambia and Malawi. If our board then voted to approve an M&A opportunity, we could call on up to $20-million more. LGT would invest $16-million of the first round, with our other investors making up the remainder, and ultimately up to $30-million, which would also be contingent on additional shareholder support. This was an increase from the $25-million they had specified in their original term sheet, and we read this as a very positive sign.

Later that night, we gathered our teams for a final debrief, during which Shakir outlined how the visit to Zambia confirmed both the risks and opportunities he had anticipated. Competition for consumers was increasing with MTN's aggressive posture, but Zoona was still a much-loved brand with a strong agent network, large consumer base and the opportunity to evolve into the kind of digital bank we envisioned. He said he had never invested before in a company that had as far to go as we did to turn overall profitable, but he so thoroughly believed in our team and vision that he had put his neck on the line to back the deal. He outlined the rest of LGT's due diligence process, which would involve an intensive period of working together to revise our financial model and create 100- and 300-day post-investment plans. If we could get investment committee approval after this modeling, their offer would be binding. LGT would then run an external due diligence with independent auditors in parallel with drafting the investment legal agreements. Shakir committed to accelerating this process to close by June, which is when we needed the cash to avoid triggering debt covenants before running dry again.

We threw all of our energy into due diligence with LGT, building out detailed operating and financial plans for our three business units. We debated every new position we needed to hire and every dollar we needed to invest. It was intense, but the collaboration with the LGT team made it feel like we were designing the future together. Shakir designated Marco as LGT deal lead, and Marco and I spoke on the phone multiple times each day, seven days a week.

One particularly complex issue emerged when Accion informed me that they wanted a partial exit of their shares from the proceeds of the investment round. Their motivation was both strategic and opportunistic. Their investment in Zoona was on Accion's balance sheet, which was managed by an independent emerging markets fintech fund that Monica had spun off, Quona Capital. It would be a great success story for both Accion and Quona to get their invested capital back while retaining their ability to share in Zoona's financial upside. But this was a tricky issue, potentially triggering similar requests from other shareholders.

I came up with a counterproposal that would let Accion cash out a quarter of their shares in Zoona in exchange for Zoona swapping shares with Accion's ownership in Socremo, the micro-finance bank in Mozambique we had been exploring as an acquisition target. I had earlier secured non-binding term sheets to purchase 60 percent of the shares from Socremo's other shareholders once our Series C closed. With my new proposal, Accion could achieve their targeted partial exit in Zoona with cash from the Series C proceeds, while still retaining their pro rata equity stake in Zoona via the share swap. Zoona would also secure a cleaner 100 percent stake in Socremo. Everyone, including LGT, agreed to move forward with this solution.

By the end of March 2018, the LGT team was ready to go to their investment committee. I felt confident despite being a bit shell-shocked by the level of adversity we had faced in the first quarter of the year. We had navigated a team restructuring, two separate bridge financing deals, a Series C term sheet negotiation and due diligence, a shareholder partial exit negotiation, and an M&A negotiation in Mozambique — all against a backdrop of a cholera epidemic and competitive attacks from two MNOs in Zambia. It was time for some good news.

On Good Friday, Shakir called to tell me that the LGT investment committee had approved the deal, subject to a couple of tweaks. I can't properly describe how good I felt after that call. We had all worked so hard for so long, and now we had approval for a $40-million investment to back our vision for the future. It was an amazing sense of validation, and once again I felt we were back on track to create a billion-dollar company that could lead the way toward a cashless Africa.

Marco told me that it was important that we accelerate our acquisition of Socremo by completing a due diligence on the bank before LGT's final investment committee meeting, scheduled for the end of May. He was also lining up a Big Four auditing firm and a technology company to audit our financials and Tachyon platform respectively, along with a financial services advisory firm called Dalberg to conduct an external commercial due diligence which would require more time from our team. He then gave me the green light to start the legal process — another confident signal that we were over the biggest hurdle — with Zoona's corporate lawyers drafting the transaction documents.

I gathered our staff and announced the milestone. Everyone cheered, and one of our employees asked when Prince Max of Liechtenstein was coming to visit. "Soon," I promised, "but first we need to close the deal." I cautioned that a deal is not a deal until the cash is in the bank, but given the intensity of the due diligence LGT had already undertaken I was confident we had a clear path to the finish line.

Who's In and Who's Out?

Having reached an agreement with us and LGT on a partial exit, Accion was out of the Series C. Likewise, Sarona would be exiting fully; they had earlier agreed to sell their remaining shares to Lundin when the round closed. With both of them out, I needed to secure confirmations from our other existing shareholders that they would participate in the round. As anticipated, there were no nasty surprises from our smaller investors: The Lundin Foundation and 4Di Capital both confirmed they were planning to put up their pro rata portions. Lundin was going through an internal restructuring to create a new investment vehicle, which meant that they would need to conduct due diligence with us in Cape Town, Zambia and Malawi despite already being a shareholder in Zoona. But their trips went smoothly, and we anticipated a positive outcome before the deal closed.

Understandably, the IFC would require more effort. Given the challenges we had faced since the IFC led our Series B round, I flew to Washington, D.C. to meet with them. The trip included a layover in Europe, during which I attended the Skoll World Forum for Social Entrepreneurship at Oxford. I caught up with Doug Galen, co-founder and CEO of our partner Rippleworks, the nonprofit that had provided us with pro bono management consulting. I shared with him our vision of evolving Zoona into a digital bank anchored by our agent network and Zoona Plus product, and updated him on our Series C round. After listening intently, Doug told me that Rippleworks was considering direct investments in ventures they supported, and suggested that Zoona could be their guinea pig. I offered Rippleworks the opportunity to participate in our Series C round, and we agreed to explore this over the next few weeks.

Following this optimistic outcome, I took a brief hop to Amsterdam. There I meet with our recently recruited independent director, Ebi Atawodi, who shared invaluable advice on launching and scaling new products from her experience of launching Uber in Nigeria and now leading their global payments team. I then returned to London to spend the weekend with Patrick Pichette, who had recently moved there. We talked about how much progress Zoona had made since our board meeting in Zambia just five months earlier, and Patrick was impressed by our pace and our ability to deal with adversity. He shared my confidence that we were on track to close our Series C round.

Patrick and I then went together to meet Sev Vettivetpillai, the new CEO of LGT, in their central London office. Marco had warmly introduced me to him on email a couple of weeks earlier. Sev had come to LGT from Abraaj, where he had been a managing partner and had worked with both Shakir and Marco. Prior to that, he had founded the African private equity fund Aureos Capital. I had read in the news that Abraaj had been in a downward spiral after their founder and CEO had been accused of misappropriating huge sums of money from their investors, including the Bill and Melinda Gates Foundation and the World Bank. But because Marco was so positive about Sev and his Africa experience, I didn't think much of it.

We were joined by Sev's new chief investment officer, Anubha Shrivastava. Sev informed us that this was Anubha's first meeting on her first day on the job at LGT, so it was excellent timing that we were all able to meet in person. I took them through our pitch deck and Patrick detailed how much he liked our team and how he had seen first-hand the adversity we had battled over the years. He also shared his view on the market and the digital products in our pipeline. Given Patrick's stature, his perspective carried plenty of weight.

Buzzing from all of these positive meetings, I finally flew to Washington, D.C. to seek confirmation of the IFC's participation in our Series C. They had been the lead investor in our Series B round, so it was important to ensure our past issues were behind us and that they signaled their ongoing support of the company. We had scaled down Mozambique and shut down the DRC, reduced our headcount in Cape Town, and even *finally* filled their board seat with a prominent financial services leader in South Africa, Shirley Maltz — all positive measures.

I knew that Seth, our IFC investment officer, was still unconvinced that we should be pursuing deposit-taking licenses and disagreed with our plans to acquire Socremo. But he was on the other side of the world and not at all dialed in to how fast the Zambian market was shifting. Moreover, he had not been part of the intensive strategy and planning conversations we were having with LGT. I had been trying my best to work with him constructively, and my trip to Washington was an opportunity to engage with his boss, Andi Dervishi, to ensure he learned the details of our Series C strategy directly from me. I respected Andi as a leading thinker of fintech in emerging markets, and was encouraged when he greeted me enthusiastically. I walked him through market developments in Zambia, our strategy to evolve into a digital bank, and the risks of relying on partners to rent deposit-taking licenses. Andi said it sounded like a well-considered path and offered his commitment that the IFC would support our round. Mission accomplished.

I then walked down the street to the Accion office. Monica wasn't in town, but I was able to meet with their chief investment officer. We reconfirmed our agreement — now written into our binding Series C term sheet with LGT — that Accion would receive a partial exit of their Zoona shares from the proceeds while Accion and Zoona would separately swap shares in

Socremo. I then walked further down the street to Omidyar Network's D.C. office and presented to their investment committee, with Arjuna and several others video-conferenced in. Afterward, Arjuna called me to confirm that Omidyar had given their approval for their full pro rata participation in our round.

My final meeting in D.C. was with Lauren Cochran from Blue Haven. I updated her on all the week's meetings, but she stopped me when I told her about LGT's new CEO, Sev Vettivetpillai. Concerned about the severity of the Abraaj misappropriation of investment funds scandal, she said she was skeptical that Abraaj's CEO was the only one involved. She asked if we still had other investors in play, but I told her we had signed an exclusivity agreement with LGT as part of their binding offer. Moreover, we desperately needed the money to launch Zoona Plus, and it would take months and even more due diligence to get another investor to the same point. The reality was that we were past the point of no return with LGT. Lauren understood our position and shifted to asking how I was doing in the midst of so much adversity — a welcome line of inquiry, given my constant state of exhaustion and stress.

Close to Closing

During a ten-hour layover in London on the way back to Cape Town, I went into the city to meet with Marco from LGT. He had been reviewing our draft legal documents and had spent days going back and forth with Seth trying to reconcile all of the IFC's idiosyncratic rights from our Series B agreement with what LGT could accept and what was best for the company. Together, we went through the IFC's rights and Seth's comments line by line; by the end of the day we had solutions to almost all outstanding issues, and he took me out to celebrate our progress.

With the external due diligence going well, shareholder commitments verbally in place and the Series C legal documents underway, we turned our attention to conducting due diligence of Socremo in Mozambique. We had been on the receiving end of many due diligence processes but had never done one ourselves, so I leaned on Marco for help. After combing through a virtual data room of documents that Socremo had made available, Marco suggested we get the Zoona, LGT and Socremo teams together in person for a meeting.

Our Zoona executive team flew to Maputo in early May, and the CEO of Socremo opened our meeting with a formal presentation on the bank's operations and financials, information we already had from the virtual data room. We were concerned that the rest of the meeting would not be the interactive discussion we had hoped for, and so Brad, who would lead the change management of the acquisition, found an opening to organize everyone into small groups. He asked each group to discuss their hopes and fears regarding the partnership, and with that the room immediately energized. The Socremo team conveyed how passionate they were about the bank and the customers they served. Some of them had been with Socremo for nearly two decades and were deeply committed to the bank's mission of serving small businesses. But they were also open and realistic about the threat facing their traditional brick-and-mortar micro-finance model, admitting that they had little idea of how to adapt to the emerging digital economy. Hence their excitement to work with Zoona.

Shakir missed the Socremo meeting, but flew in late that night and was debriefed by the LGT team. The next day, he revealed to me that our deal was under pressure because of Zoona's recent financial performance. Despite our foundational improvements, Zoona was still losing about $500,000 per month, driven by the cholera epidemic, increased competition and our recent money transfer price reduction in Zambia. I talked him through the cost-cutting measures we had implemented, our laser focus on due diligence all year, and the need to get the Series C closed so that we could free ourselves from the cash-flow straitjacket and get back to executing our plan. Shakir was understanding, but said it would be challenging to communicate this to the brand-new senior management team that Sev had brought with him, as they had not been involved in the prior discussions. He was also clear that this was his problem and not mine.

We organized a Zoona and LGT meeting later in the day, during which we dove into our operational challenges and all we were doing to navigate them. Brad presented data on positive early trends we were seeing from our money transfer price reduction, with previously churned consumers coming back to us. Brett shared the significant progress we had made getting Zoona Plus ready for launch in the third quarter, along with new enterprise payment commercial deals underway with two major banks in Zambia. The LGT team noted that we had weathered a perfect storm and thanked us for our transparency; they now felt confident they would be able to effectively communicate the current situation to their investment committee.

Later that night, Arjuna called me to let me know that Omidyar Network had approved an $800,000 advance of their pro rata investment portion to help alleviate our cash-flow pressure. I had been worried that we might breach our debt covenants earlier than planned — and before our Series C closed — because of our price reduction, so this was a huge relief. Omidyar had come through for us once again.

The mood was upbeat when we parted ways with the LGT team at Maputo's Mavalane International Airport. We would see each other again in two weeks in London, where LGT was holding their final investment committee meeting and we had scheduled our board meeting. It felt like we could all see the finish line.

A fortnight later, when I finally made my way to Cape Town International Airport to board the flight to London, I called Marco. He congratulated me with the news that LGT's deal team had made a formal recommendation to proceed with the investment. While he couldn't guarantee the outcome, his last words to me were, "I expect you will have a much less anxious flight back to Cape Town."

The return flight, as it turned out, would be the most anxious of my life.

Things Fall Apart

On landing at Heathrow just after 6 a.m. the next morning, I opened my email while standing in the immigration queue to find a devastating message from Seth. The IFC would not be participating in our Series C, he wrote, but he promised to "help as much as I can to close the round as anticipated."

What. The. Fuck.

Yes, we had a rocky past, but I had had a verbal in-person assurance from Andi Dervishi, Seth's boss at the IFC, just a few weeks earlier that they would participate. If LGT caught wind of this news ahead of their investment committee meeting in just a few hours, it would upset all the complex arrangements we had reached and could jeopardize the entire investment round.

I messaged our board chair, Monica, and she called me immediately. Her response was the same as mine. She advised me to call Andi to figure out what was going on. She nervously reassured me we would get through this setback and, with LGT's pro forma approval, we could figure out how to get the IFC back to the table.

I then met Arjuna at Omidyar Network's London office and shared the news with him. He usually had a decent poker face but this time he was clearly shocked. Just as we were sitting down to talk, my phone rang; I saw Shakir's name on my caller ID so I excused myself to answer.

"Listen, Mike," Shakir said, with a shaky voice. "I have some bad news. LGT's investment committee has turned down the deal. I feel like absolute shit about this. I think it's the wrong decision but I couldn't convince them otherwise. I'm really sorry."

I was in shock. The rest of the call was a blur, but I do remember him telling me there was a chance he could rustle up $1-2-million from their affiliated LGT Venture Philanthropy entity. He also told me he had canceled his flight to London for the celebratory dinner that LGT had arranged for our board. I shared this news with Arjuna and, after a protracted silence he gave me a hug and tried to reassure me that we would work it out at the board meeting the next day.

I was not reassured.

I walked like a zombie through central London for more than an hour, returning to my shoebox-sized hotel room to call Brad, Brett and Keith. Brett and Keith were on their way to Cape Town International Airport to catch their flight to London, while Brad was at home, planning to conference in remotely. As they tried to digest the news, Keith and Brett asked if they should still come to London or if they should literally drive back to the office to start cutting staff. I told them to get on the plane because the tickets were already paid for and we needed to problem-solve this with our board and investors. Later, I wrote an emotional email to Andi and Seth from the IFC, expressing my shock at the news of their decision and notifying them that LGT was following suit, both of which put our company on the verge of collapse.

When Keith and Brett arrived the next morning, they were as somber as I was. Together, we headed to the Omidyar Network office for our board meeting. Ebi flew in from Amsterdam to join us in person, while Brad, Shirley and Patrick dialed in by phone. Monica, who had flown in from Washington, D.C., arrived a few minutes late having managed to arrange breakfast with Anubha, LGT's new CIO, to try to find out what had happened.

It turned out that LGT's investment committee had reviewed the Dalberg external due diligence report — which highlighted the increasing competition in Zambia, along with our poor year-to-date financial results due to the cholera epidemic and money transfer price reduction — and decided to walk away. The news that their investment committee meeting barely lasted a few minutes — after four months of intensive due diligence — hit me like a freight train.

Patrick somberly noted that it was the board's fiduciary duty to consider options for a quick sale of the company. Everyone looked at me, and it was one of the few times in my life when I didn't know what to say.

Quick Turnaround

Thankfully, Arjuna came to my rescue and suggested we push LGT for as much money as we could get. If our existing investors would still pitch in $5-million as planned, *maybe* we could find one or two new investors and get the round back up to $10–15-million. This would be enough to get us on stable footing in Zambia. Everyone agreed, and at the end of the meeting I called Shakir. I told him that our shareholders would put in $5-million if LGT would put in $5-million, and we could thereby salvage the round. Otherwise, there was a good chance Zoona would have to be quickly sold or go bankrupt — bad news for everyone. He promised to do his best.

Early the next morning, Shakir got back to me, this time in a more optimistic tone. He told me he had spoken to Sev, LGT's CEO, about our board's request for $5-million and managed to arrange a meeting with me at their London office at 11 a.m.

I met Marco outside the LGT office; he was clearly as shell-shocked as I was. Like us, he had led a deal team that had worked day and night, and wanted to move forward as badly as we did. But the decision was not his to make. We went up to the meeting room and nervously took our seats as LGT's chief investment officer, Anubha, walked in. She apologized for Sev's absence; he couldn't make the meeting but she assured me she had spoken to him. With Shakir joining us via phone from Nairobi, Anubha dove straight in, peppering me with questions which I took as an encouraging sign, as she could have just told me why they were walking away. Her questioning lasted more than 90 minutes, and when she was done she shifted to a more positive tone, explaining that LGT was indeed planning to move forward with a $5-million investment in Zoona from LGT Venture Philanthropy. There were still some hoops to jump through, though, as we would need to prepare a new business plan for a smaller round, and the LGT Venture Philanthropy board would also need to sign off. But given how much time LGT had invested in the deal, they wanted to find a solution, even though they stood by their decision to not invest the $30-million.

This felt like a breakthrough. With $5-million from LGT, I knew we could secure another $5-million from our shareholders and make a plan. I left with Marco to meet Brett and Keith in a nearby bar. They had been messaging me without response every 10 minutes during the meeting, and when I told them LGT had committed $5-million they both bear-hugged Marco and me. It was a moment of pure joy considering that we had all thought Zoona was dead just 24 hours earlier.

I informed our board and investors, to everyone's great relief, and told them we would need to move quickly on their planned pro rata investments because the shift to LGT Venture Philanthropy could delay the close by two months. I knew Monica had the biggest challenge ahead because Accion was expecting to get money *out* of the planned Series C round, rather than put more money *in*, but she assured me she was on it.

New Game Plan

Brett, Keith and I flew back to Cape Town and met with Brad to coordinate an action plan. All M&A activities would be cut. Instead of arranging our own deposit-taking licenses in Zambia and Malawi, we would need to rely on partners. This shift in strategy meant we could make some material cuts to our overheads to make the smaller investment last until we became profitable.

The following day we presented the news to our unsuspecting staff. Instead of a slow, formal downsizing process, as we had undertaken in the past, we offered a voluntary redundancy package to the entire company. To avoid losing key people, we offered stock options to those we most wanted to retain. We also began to build a new financial plan. After several iterations with the LGT deal team over the course of a few days, the plan was ready for their investment committee. I also negotiated a new term sheet with Shakir and Marco and we agreed to drop the pre-money valuation from $70-million to $65-million — a largely symbolic gesture to help push the deal over the line.

Meanwhile, I was pushing all of our shareholders to secure the additional $5-million. Omidyar Network had already advanced us $800,000 and had approval for more, but would invest only as much as Accion. They wanted to be sure that Accion would reverse their partial exit stance and put money into the company. Lundin had a procedural hiccup linked to their new fund set-up, and their new investment committee now couldn't meet until early July. But they were encouraged that LGT had come back to the table and signaled a positive outcome. 4Di Capital agreed to quickly advance their pro rata funds in June to help us avoid breaching our debt covenants.

The IFC was still a sticking point. I shared our new plan with Seth, including the absence of M&A, which I thought he would like given how much more prudent it was. He had cited the IFC's lack of belief in our M&A strategy as one of the reasons they had decided not to participate, along with our failure to deliver on our Series B expansion into Mozambique. (Whether these were the true reasons, I do not know. Much later I heard from several people, including a member of the IFC fintech investment team, that there were major internal budget shifts within the IFC at the time that affected their investment decisions.) We now had a plan for a scaled-down business focused on Zambia and Malawi and geared toward profitability, which should have been music to their ears. Our other shareholders were stepping up, and Accion promised they would do their part, provided the IFC did theirs. Besides, we were only asking the IFC for $750,000, a tiny number on their huge balance sheet.

Seth came back to me with more bad news: The IFC was *still* not going to invest. My heart sank. I had not yet told LGT about the IFC's earlier decision because I had been hoping they would ultimately step up. But now I had to disclose it. I also knew that without the IFC's participation, Accion would be nervous about investing, which would in turn be a problem for Omidyar Network — and we would be back to square one.

Seth tried to reassure me that the IFC was committed to helping our round close, which I found hard to believe. I shifted tactics and told him that if the IFC wasn't going to participate, then they should lose all of their key shareholder rights, including their board seat and veto rights on future financing. If I could get the IFC to agree to these concessions, then I could disclose the bad news to LGT with the caveat that the IFC would also become a marginalized and passive shareholder going forward. This could be positioned positively, given our rocky history with them. Seth was hesitant but agreed to take a proposal to the IFC's investment committee. After several iterations, we chopped and changed our existing shareholders' agreement, and Seth was able to get approval for all of the main changes I had requested.

Meanwhile, I went back to Doug Galen at Rippleworks, who was sitting on a soaring Ripple cryptocurrency endowment and wanted to help us. Ironically, the fact that LGT had pulled out made it easier for Rippleworks to invest because they had a mandate to provide "faith capital" to high-impact startups that couldn't easily access commercial capital. We now fit this niche, and a $3-million investment from Rippleworks would more than make up for the hole left by the IFC. We were Rippleworks's first proposed investment, which meant they had some internal processes to navigate, but I was encouraged that this might be a possibility. I could also share with LGT that even without the IFC, we could still get the required $5-million to match their investment.

A few days later, Shakir called to tell me he had received approval from the LGT Venture Philanthropy board for the $5-million, but with a few caveats. Because $5-million was significantly higher than LGT Venture Philanthropy's normal investments, they wanted to split it into two tranches — $3-million plus $2-million. The second tranche would be contingent on a performance milestone, and though LGT would underwrite it, they wanted to find a new investor to backfill their funds so that LGT ended up with only $3-million of exposure. On top of this, LGT still wanted a board seat along with a harsh redemption right that stated if we weren't profitable within eighteen months they could unilaterally force a liquidation of their shares.

I didn't like any of these terms. We had strayed too far from the original deal, and finding another investor to backfill the second tranche could be difficult. They also wanted the same amount of influence and control despite shrinking their exposure by 90 percent. I was, however, pragmatic enough to realize that we had absolutely no choice but to agree; we needed their money to get everyone else's money, and without all of that money Zoona would die. My only pushback to Shakir was that I wanted the second tranche milestone to be based on reducing our monthly fixed salary expenses, which I knew we could control given the round of cuts that were already in motion.

I also finally informed Shakir that the IFC would not be participating. I explained that they had conceded their key shareholder rights and board seat, and that I had quadrupled the IFC's missing pro rata share by sourcing $3-million from Rippleworks. I stressed that having the IFC as a passive investor without any material veto rights was in the best interests of the company and the shareholders. Even if the IFC wanted to invest, I preferred the outcome I had negotiated. Shakir told me that if I had disclosed this earlier, LGT would have walked away because it was important to them that the IFC, leader of our Series B round, continued its support. But he understood why I had held back this information and appreciated that I had done my best to bring him a solution instead of just a problem. He said he would have to go back to the LGT Venture Philanthropy board with the disclosure, but was cautiously optimistic.

Luckily, the concessions from the IFC and the new money from Rippleworks proved to be enough, and LGT Venture Philanthropy signed the new term sheet. Rippleworks approved their $3-million investment and we instructed our law firm to update the legal documents with the new terms.

The Downward Spiral

As we entered July, our severance packages kicked in, with several high-profile staff departures that would have been unthinkable six weeks earlier. My former executive team, at that stage under Brad — including our CMO Lelemba Phiri and CTO Andre Penderis — had all agreed to exit packages. With our entire marketing, communications and agent performance management team being made redundant and M&A plans put on ice, there was no alternative. Brett took back control of our technology team and our leadership team was once again the original four — Brad, Brett, Keith and I — plus Shungu. She stayed on as our chief regulatory officer, playing an important role in supporting our downsizing efforts, before exiting herself a few months later to pursue a new opportunity.

I also had to convey the bad news to Socremo, and their three institutional shareholders with whom I had negotiated and signed term sheets, that our acquisition wouldn't be going forward. It was embarrassing and damaging to my credibility, but it was a reality. I tried to stay positive and keep our options open for a future commercial partnership.

We still needed approval on participation from Lundin, who were finally ready for their investment committee meeting after setting up a new fund structure. I hadn't imagined the outcome was in question, given how supportive they had been and how smoothly their due diligence had gone. But Lundin's managing director, Stephen Nairne, called me to say their investment committee had not yet voted to participate. A primary concern was the IFC's decision to withdraw. He told me, however, that it was not a *no*, just not a *yes*, and he would go back to the committee with more information on our updated plans, as they evolved. However, their next meeting wouldn't take place for at least a month.

Meanwhile, Monica was preparing for the tough job of asking Accion's investment committee for their unexpected participation in our round, while requesting that the funds be disbursed immediately to relieve our cash-flow pressure. I relayed the news from Lundin, specifically stressing that they didn't explicitly say no, and that I was confident we could get them to say yes after we brought them up to speed on all the progress we had made in the past few weeks. But this would take more time. I also noted that we were still on track with LGT for their $5-million, and that I had received LGT's full comments on our updated legal agreements, a promising sign that we were once again getting close.

In the midst of all this, I started picking up on judgemental comments about Zoona and my implied leadership from every angle and all quarters: About how misguided our M&A strategy was, how we had built too big a team, how we always tried to do too much, how we were too slow launching new products, how we had a culture of frivolous spending, how we didn't give enough freedom to our top talent to execute, how we had neglected our core agent network and money transfer consumers, how we had underestimated the competition in Zambia, how we never should have gone into Mozambique, how we should have foreseen LGT's and the IFC's and Lundin's non-approvals earlier, how we didn't treat our investors as partners and always expected them to bail us out... Everyone had an opinion and I absorbed every one of them personally. But what they didn't see was that I was my own harshest critic, and it was impossible to escape the persistent thought that I had fucked everything up.

Then, almost as an omen, my dog Zoona died. Isabelle and I had named him Zoona as a puppy nine years before, when the company was still called Mobile Transactions and the word "Zoona" — *It's real* — had resonated so strongly with us. He had severe spinal arthritis, common in German Shepherds, and was in pain all the time. I drove him to the vet and stroked the top of his head while the vet administered the lethal dose. When he took his last breath, I broke down in tears.

Even though I'm known as a perpetually positive person, to say this was a really shitty time is a huge understatement.

LGT Pulls Out... Again

Monica had warned me that Accion's approval was not guaranteed, so I was extremely anxious. With Accion's participation, Omidyar Network would match, Lundin would likely come in, and LGT and Rippleworks would close.

Without it, the house of cards would almost certainly collapse. When she messaged me with good news from Accion's investment committee, I breathed a huge sigh of relief. LGT's commitment of $5-million and the IFC's concessions for their non-participation had been enough to get Accion over the line. Accion also agreed to advance the full amount, which we would need to pay out severance packages from our staff cuts. I relayed the news to Stephen at Lundin, and he said he would move up Lundin's investment committee meeting by a couple of weeks to the first week of August to try for an approval again.

On my next call with LGT, I was surprised that their chief investment officer, Anubha, joined along with Marco, Shakir and the LGT deal team. We had full approval from both the LGT investment committee and LGT Venture Philanthropy board, so Anubha's presence on the call was a red flag. She wanted to know why our money transfer results were trending downwards and I reiterated the reasons, stressing that we had been stuck in LGT due diligence all year with few levers to pull without the round closing, and outlining our strategy and plan for when it did. The only thing we could do in the meantime was cut costs, and in this regard we were ahead of plan.

She then asked whether Zoona's valuation of $65-million was still fair, implying that she expected it to come down. But we had negotiated terms with LGT multiple times already — including dropping the valuation just a month earlier — and I already had advances from Omidyar Network, Accion, 4Di and Blue Haven in our bank account, along with full approval from Rippleworks (contingent on LGT closing). It seemed unfair that we had been pushed by LGT into a corner and then asked to drop our valuation right before we were meant to close — for the second time. I also mentioned that Lundin's formal approval was still pending, but added that

Rippleworks's $3-million commitment was more than we were originally expecting from the IFC and Lundin combined, and also that the IFC had made material concessions for their non-participation. The LGT team then unexpectedly informed me that they would halt their process until Lundin's approval came through. They said they expected all of our existing shareholders to invest in the round; they had already made an exception for the IFC but were not prepared to do this again.

I was shattered. I called Arjuna, and for the first time I admitted out loud that LGT was not the right fit for our business. I had worked day and night for months to close our Series C, but now I suspected that even if we did close, all of this baggage would carry over just as it had with the IFC after Series B. Arjuna suggested we hear from Rippleworks on the situation, so I sent Doug Galen a long email about what was happening and how I was reconsidering whether or not LGT was the right fit. He responded immediately, affirming that Rippleworks could consider coming in without LGT. This was very generous, especially considering we were their first ever investment.

A few days later, I had another call with the LGT deal team and Anubha. They were preparing to go back to their investment committee one final time. I asked for certainty on their position, and shared that I had secured verbal commitment from Rippleworks on their $3-million and that Lundin had moved up their investment committee meeting to the following week for their $1-million. The call ended much more positively than the previous one.

The next morning, Marco called me with a proposal. He thought that we might be able to finally get the deal over the line if LGT's $5-million investment was structured as convertible debt instead of equity. This would eliminate their concern on valuation and give us time to execute our plan before finding a new lead investor. He followed this idea up with some terms that I thought could work.

Just a few hours later, Shakir called me.

"Mike, I have bad news," he said. "We aren't going to get there. I'm sorry."

By now I wasn't angry or sad. I felt relief.

EMBRACING FAILURE: WHAT I LEARNED

My prime frustration looking back on this period was how much cash flow and investor challenges dominated my everyday life. This constant search for life-sustaining investment was at times exhilarating — and there was great satisfaction and meaning to be had when a deal closed and funds hit our bank account — but it was completely exhausting. Moreover, it distracted me from actually building our business in service to our agents and consumers, which is what I wanted to focus on. I was aware of the dilemma at the time, but I couldn't escape it, because we were completely dependent on closing the next round of investment and it was my responsibility to deliver on this. Ultimately, I failed to do that.

What makes this an even harder pill to swallow was that I genuinely felt we were poised for takeoff. We had a battle-tested team and culture, an ambitious strategy with major strategic opportunities, and a brand-new technology platform and digital product set that was the best in the market. Combined with our agent network, consumer base and strong brand, this should have been enough to close a Series C investment round and keep us in the game.

If our Series C investment had closed, we would have had a war chest to cut our money transfer prices, which I believe would have fended off the intensifying competition from MTN and Airtel and bought us the time we needed to recover from the cholera crisis and fully transition our consumer base to Zoona Plus. We also would have been able to apply for our own deposit-taking license in Zambia to enable us to expand Zoona Plus countrywide.

I also believe the Socremo acquisition would have worked. It might have been prudent to postpone it until Zambia was stabilized, but even if we had done nothing but purchase the shares, we would have owned a stable and profitable asset that we could have planned to transform later. It was a great pity we never had the opportunity to try.

The inherent vulnerability of our position was that we needed a Series C investment merely to survive. The roots of this problem dated back two years, with our failed expansion approach to Mozambique and the rapid scaling up of our Cape Town headcount and operating costs. If we had run a leaner business focused on Zambia and Malawi instead, we would have been able to raise a Series C from a much stronger position and under less pressure.

In hindsight, I would have targeted Series C investors differently. We wasted a lot of time courting large private equity investors, all of whom were enthralled by what we had built and our vision for the future. But ultimately we didn't fit their model of only investing in already profitable companies; that we had transparently communicated that we weren't yet profitable was beside the point. We would have been better off either targeting impact investors for one more (smaller) round or trying to entice a global venture capital investor who was willing to take more risk to fund our transition from an over-the-counter money transfer business to a digital bank. The latter would have been a more feasible option if we were in a bigger market, but would have been a tough sell in Zambia and Malawi.

As for LGT, it's unfortunate their senior management team and investment strategy changed so late in the process, and that they dragged things out as long as they did, which compounded our problems and delayed our acting on them. Perhaps our timing in dealing with LGT was unfortunate. Their new senior team didn't last long; a year later they were disbanded and Sev Vettivetpillai was charged for his role in the

Abraaj private equity scandal shortly before he joined LGT; he subsequently pleaded guilty in an extradition deal with the U.S. authorities.

It turned out we had chosen the wrong lead investor; we should have taken any of the other offers on the table, even though the terms weren't comparable. To be fair, though, it would have been difficult to justify this decision at the time. We had developed a strong connection to LGT's deal team, who genuinely believed in our potential and had signaled strongly that they were prepared to back us. I just wish we hadn't needed their money so badly.

CHAPTER 10

FAILING TO EXIT

With our Series C collapsing, I started thinking seriously about whether I was the right CEO to take Zoona forward. I knew I wasn't the only one wondering this, with the whispers in the corridors amplifying those inside my head. Patrick coached me that life is long and it wouldn't be the end of the world if Zoona failed, encouraging me that I would have another shot as an entrepreneur. He also re-emphasized that we should seriously consider selling the company before it was too late.

As much as I could *hear* Patrick's words in my head, though, I couldn't yet *feel* them in my heart. After climbing the mountain for more than nine years, I had finally caught a glimpse of the summit — albeit momentarily before a new storm blew in. Why should we throw in the towel and give up now just because an investor had pulled out? We were the same founding team with the same strategy that just a few months ago everyone was lauding. Our brand was loved, Zoona Plus was just hitting the market in Zambia, and our Malawi business was still thriving. Shouldn't we instead hunker down, find a new lead investor to recapitalize and try for another summit attempt?

I thought back to the classic definition of entrepreneurship coined by Harvard Professor Emeritus Howard Stevenson: *"The pursuit of opportunity beyond resources controlled."* I lived by this mantra. The opportunity in front of us was still very real, and I couldn't bring myself to step aside without doing everything I could to give Zoona another chance.

This decision to keep going would become a fateful one. It would lead us down a path where I would face one of the hardest dilemmas of my life and learn that sometimes the best — and hardest — act of leadership is knowing when to exit.

Farewell, Keith

We still had some life in us. Almost ironically, the Lundin approval for their $1-million came through at the beginning of August 2018, shortly after LGT pulled out for the second time. Rippleworks had their $3-million on standby, but now we had a new problem: There was no one to lead the round and set the terms — a fact that Seth pointed out when he made us aware that all of the concessions the IFC had made assumed an LGT investment and thus were no longer valid. I was incredulous, given that our other investors had advanced funds to help the company through a crisis, some specifically on the understanding that the IFC's preferred shareholder rights, including their veto on future financing, would be neutralized due to its non-participation in the round.

To overcome the stalemate, Monica thankfully volunteered to lead on behalf of Accion. After consulting our other investors, we decided to structure the round as convertible debt on the eleventh-hour terms that Marco and I had frantically aligned on (but LGT did not ultimately approve), retrofitting all the previous convertible debt advances to these same terms. My goal was simply to get the cash in as urgently as possible to pay committed severances for staff exits and avoid triggering any senior debt covenants, which would compound our pain.

Plus, I knew I wasn't in any position to negotiate. I was still hopeful, though, that our business was strong enough to find a new lead equity investor by the end of the year — even on a reduced valuation — to convert all of these convertible debt notes to equity.

Finally, we had some closure on what had been a long, harrowing and extremely draining process. Our $40-million round had shrunk to $7.5-million, with $3.5-million advanced and already spent, and we needed to make the fresh $4-million from Lundin and Rippleworks count. As part of the new terms, the founders were stripped of a voting board seat to give the investors more control, while Lundin and Rippleworks gained board observer seats. Our board would also start having discussions at each meeting without Brad, Brett, Keith or me in the room. Language was also included in the legal agreements to require us to find a strategic partner that could set the stage for a sale. It was amazing how much had changed in just three months.

Perhaps Patrick was right — we had had a good run, but maybe we were approaching the end of the road.

Keith was the first to see it. He had spent every waking minute for nine months alongside me trying to close our Series C. He had carried the brunt of the due diligence load and then, after LGT pulled out for the second time, he was consumed with laying off staff and cutting costs as deeply and quickly as possible. After he took some well-earned leave, I wrote him a long email, detailing the business and cash-flow challenges still ahead, and what would be required from him as CFO. I had no doubt he could do the job, I wrote, but given how burnt out he was, did he still want it?

Keith responded immediately: "Easy answer, Mike. It's exit time for me."

When we met a week later, I could see the burden had lifted from his shoulders. He was at peace with his decision and was intent on leaving on the best possible terms, while setting the company up for the next phase. It was a bittersweet departure; we had been through so many ups and downs together and were also close friends. But I knew it was the right decision for Keith and his family.

From B2C to B2B

When we announced Keith's exit at a company staff meeting, the tears flowed. He had always been a bedrock of stability amid the chaos, and all of our staff looked up to him. We gave him a fitting send-off, and then Brad, Brett and I regrouped. It was as if we had gone back in time to our origins, with the three of us trying to figure out what to do next to stay alive.

We acknowledged that without a Series C we didn't have deep enough pockets — not to mention the regulatory license — to properly scale Zoona Plus and compete against the MNOs on a business-to-consumer (B2C) strategy. It made sense, then, when Brett proposed pivoting to become the business-to-business (B2B) fintech platform that he had envisioned from the very beginning when Zoona was still Mobile Transactions. This time, with our newly released Tachyon platform, both our technology and the market seemed ready. We could offer enterprise bulk payment services to banks and corporates, and partner with other emerging agent and merchant acquiring networks to expand our cash-in and cash-out points beyond just Zoona agents. In time, we could even spin off or sell our agent network to focus on scaling our technology platform in Zambia and Malawi and taking it into new markets.

A natural starting point for this strategy was to target the corporate divisions of banks that serviced payments for all the big companies, donors and government agencies. There were only about a thousand ATMs in all of Zambia, always with long lines of people, especially after pay day at the end of the month. In aggregate, hundreds of millions of dollars of cash would flow from ATMs to consumers each month, since Zambia was still very much a cash economy and electronic merchant payments were very niche. Many of the banks wanted to reduce their expensive ATM footprints (not to mention close even more expensive branches), which required electricity and cash-in-transit services that were harder to provide outside of city centers. In Kenya, where M-Pesa had transformed the market, banks were shifting almost entirely to agent networks for cash-in and cash-out, providing a model for the future.

It quickly became apparent that this B2B value proposition was strong. We signed contracts with several corporate banking divisions, along with Kazang, an established merchant aggregator company that had more than 6,000 point-of-sale devices in the market. The technical integrations moved much more slowly, but led to an unexpected opportunity from Atlas Mara, one of Zambia's largest retail banks with a footprint across the continent. Atlas Mara was preparing to launch their own consumer mobile wallet called Tenga to compete with the MNOs, and wanted to use Zoona agents — and by extension Kazang merchants — to provide cash-in and cash-out. We signed a contract and integrated platforms at a surprising pace, and added Tenga branding to our agent kiosks with a "powered by Zoona" tagline.

Other big retail banks then came calling. Barclays Zambia had begun to fear they would get left behind in the rapidly changing consumer market, and expressed interest in using our

Zoona Plus product set but with their branding (an approach known as white-labelling). Zanaco, Zambia's market-leading retail bank, explored the possibility of buying Zoona Zambia outright (ironically after hiring a senior leader from MTN who had been a key driver behind the agent carpet-bombing strategy that gained MTN market share but apparently left a huge operational mess that he didn't want to repeat). Both options were appealing to consider, but the practical implementations were more challenging: Barclays was at the start of a large and time-consuming rebrand to Absa, having earlier announced a strategic withdrawal from Africa, and Zanaco wanted to enter into an intensive due diligence led by a third party before committing to anything. We had just come out of months of due diligence with LGT and had no appetite or capacity for more. Moreover, it would have exposed our prized money transfer product heading into a death spiral, making a successful outcome far from certain. After considering our partnership options, we figured Atlas Mara was our best bet since it was both the fastest and non-exclusive; once we gained traction with them and stabilized, we could always circle back to other banks later.

Meanwhile, in Malawi...

Despite our troubles in Zambia, business was booming next door in Malawi. In October 2018, we had reached 175,000 monthly active consumers transacting more than $10-million per month through 600 franchise agents. The majority of this value was generated from paying out Mukuru international money transfers from South Africa and had been achieved with minimal growth in operating expenses, making Zoona Malawi an increasingly profitable standalone business.

The Mukuru growth had been catalyzed by a game-changing partnership that Brett and his enterprise payment deputy, Bridgid Thomson, had struck earlier with First Capital Bank (FCB), the third-largest retail bank in Malawi. FCB was now using the Zoona platform to enable our agents to trade electronic float for cash instantly at any of their forty branches. Prior to this, agents would have to wait hours for funds to clear through the banking system while their customers, many of whom had walked long distances from their villages to receive their Mukuru money transfers, waited patiently for them to return from the bank with cash. After rolling out the FCB partnership, Mukuru's monthly payout value in Malawi immediately spiked and grew sustainably thereafter; industry NGO FinMark Trust later reported that the South Africa-Malawi corridor saw the highest growth in formal remittance transaction value among Southern African Development Community (SADC) countries during the period that correlated exactly with our FCB partnership[1]. In fact, on Christmas Eve 2018, there were so many Zoona agent electronic float-for-cash transactions due to Mukuru pay-out demand that FCB branches ran out of cash nationwide!

As Brad and Brett started to drive our B2B pivot, I continued to pitch frantically to investors to try to find a new Series C lead to replace LGT and convert all of our convertible debt. But after many promising starts, I was getting nowhere; in our state of flux, we were seen as simply too much of a risk. On top of that our USD cash runway was shortening faster than we had forecasted, with a déjà vu depreciation of the Zambian kwacha (reducing our USD revenue) unluckily coinciding with a rare

---

[1] *South Africa to the Rest of SADC Remittance Pricing Report* (FinMark Trust); available at finmark.org.za

strengthening of the South African rand (increasing our USD expenses). After considering our limited options for a cash injection, I proposed to our board that we try to sell Zoona Malawi. In addition to harvesting some cash and living to fight another day in our Zambia home market, we could use this as proof of concept for our B2B strategy by selling our Malawi agent network but retaining our technology platform for enterprise payment partnerships.

I flew to Blantyre and pitched the opportunity to the CEO of FCB. I proposed that FCB would gain our Malawi agent network (to rebrand as their own), consumer base and revenue streams, while Zoona would gain cash and keep a smaller recurring revenue stream as a B2B technology partner so that the agents still used the Zoona platform. Zoona and FCB would also be strategic partners for acquiring future enterprise payment clients with a shared revenue model. The CEO and his head of corporate banking were receptive, but were also deep into other deals and would need time — something we unfortunately didn't have much of. To get started, though, they agreed to begin a technical integration and sign a commercial partnership agreement, the first step toward a possible acquisition later.

I also reached out to Paul Maasdorp from Emerging Capital Partners (ECP), a private equity fund that had run an extensive due diligence on Zoona for our Series C round, but declined to make an offer because we were not profitable at a group level. ECP was also a major shareholder in Mukuru, with Paul a director on their board. Paul understood the strategic importance of Zoona to Mukuru, so I pitched him the opportunity for ECP to replace LGT and lead an investment round with a $5-million ticket — a small amount for ECP that I framed as an entry point to build up to a longer-term partnership and possible greater investment later. In the process, I probably over-shared about Zoona's troubles.

Paul confirmed afterwards that he was interested in exploring an investment in Zoona and asked for a due diligence pack to review. He later called me wearing his Mukuru hat and floated the idea that it would be easier and preferable if Mukuru could just buy Zoona Malawi outright. Zoona was by far the biggest payout channel for Mukuru in Malawi, which was a large and growing market for them, and if Zoona went down it would be a major problem. He also told me that the Mukuru board, which consisted of Paul and the Mukuru founders, was now concerned about their dependency on Zoona since our series C had collapsed, and had tasked Mukuru's management to consider how to de-risk their Malawi payout channel.

I informed Zoona's board that I was pursuing these two tracks with FCB and Mukuru, but I wanted to get at least one more option on the table to give us more negotiating leverage and the best chances of a favorable deal. I flew to Malawi again and, along with our managing director Killy Kanjo, went to pitch to the country's two MNOs, Airtel and TNM. As with FCB, I offered to sell our Malawi entity including our agent network and consumer base for cash, with Zoona remaining in the market as a B2B technology partner. I also pitched to Mukuru's direct competitors in South Africa, which were eyeing the growing Malawi remittance corridor but lacked pay-out channels. Everyone was receptive, but with the Christmas break approaching it would be difficult for anyone to move quickly.

The Mukuru Offer

Late in the evening before a Zoona board meeting at the end of November 2018, I received an email with a non-binding offer from Mukuru to purchase Zoona Malawi. It was an offer, at least, but it wasn't nearly as good as I had hoped it would be and there were numerous caveats. They had sent it late, having been aware of our board meeting for weeks, and set an acceptance deadline that expired in just a few days, which put pressure on us.

Mukuru had read the mood of Zoona's investors better than I. At the board meeting, we had a sobering conversation in which it became clear that Mukuru's offer was the only option that mattered because it was the only one on paper. I didn't disagree that we should consider it, but I didn't want Zoona to be manoeuvred into a position where it only had one option, and I believed that the other options I was pursuing would materialize with a little more time. More time required more investment, however, and there was still no appetite for that from our shareholders. I was given some leeway to negotiate, but that was that.

I left that board meeting more downcast than I'd ever been before, even after our Series C collapsed. For the first time, I told Isabelle out loud that I thought my Zoona days were numbered. Perhaps I should have been happy that we had an offer, which is what I had been working toward — but I wasn't. The predicament we were in was slowly dawning on me: After years of being a trailblazing startup that investors were chasing with money, now nobody would touch us, and even our own shareholders had closed their checkbooks. Our entire future had become dependent on closing an uncertain deal that we were being pressured into, and even if we did we would still be saddled with $6-million of senior debt and $7.5-million of convertible debt that we could never repay without a major equity infusion. To rub salt in the wound, an emergency impact bridge investor I was counting on turned us down, citing a lack of confidence that their investment would give us enough runway to sort out all of our troubles.

After a week of moping, I pulled myself together. I pushed back on Mukuru's deadline and signaled that they weren't the only company interested, which shifted the dynamics positively for us. Paul, who continued to lead the negotiation, reaffirmed Mukuru's intention to move quickly in good faith to close a deal with us, citing their desire to protect their Malawi business. I countered their offer by proposing that we realize fair cash value for Zoona Malawi while also retaining an ongoing partnership as a B2B technology provider, since they didn't have their own agent management platform (and we weren't proposing to sell them ours). Mukuru agreed, and over a series of phone calls between Christmas and New Year's they materially improved their offer. We reached an agreement on non-binding terms, with a roadmap to make them binding by February 15 after a brief due diligence, and then a swift process to close by March 2019. Suddenly things were starting to look up again, and after a short break I regained my optimism about the future and parked any lingering self-doubts about my role as CEO.

The due diligence with Mukuru went as smoothly as any we had ever experienced. We had a well-run, profitable business in Malawi, and it helped that Mukuru knew both Zoona and the Malawi market well. When Paul emailed me to say they needed a short extension to the February 15 deadline to wrap things up before extending us a binding offer, I thought little of it given the positive relationships that had begun to gel. They had started their due diligence late because of the extra time in early January we had taken to finalize the term sheet negotiation, he explained, and I knew their side was working as hard as ours. I indicated that any time before the end of February would be fine to receive their binding offer.

We had a more optimistic first quarter board meeting. Everyone seemed positive and excited about our fledgling B2B strategy and the imminent infusion of cash that would fuel us for another go. As expected, our cash position was tightening, though: We projected that we had enough cash to survive until the end of April — our cash cliff date since the previous convertible debt closed — but not beyond that. To make matters worse, I informed the board we were going to breach one of our senior debt covenants at the end of the month, along with receiving a request from MicroVest, our biggest senior lender, for a partial early principal repayment out of the sale proceeds from Mukuru to reduce their Zoona exposure.

In an about-turn from our previous board meeting made possible by the imminent Malawi sale, Omidyar Network, Accion and Lundin signaled willingness to go back to their investment committees and ask for money to bridge us until the Mukuru deal closed. Regarding the debt covenant breach and early repayment request, the board decided that our lenders would have to hold on because we didn't want to agree to anything now, especially if our shareholders needed to invest more cash. MicroVest was disappointed with the response, but also understood this reasonable position. They reaffirmed their support of the business and agreed to postpone their repayment request for now, while reiterating that it would be back on the table as soon as we closed with Mukuru.

In the final days of February, I received an email from Mukuru with what I thought would be a binding offer. But it was much weaker than we'd previously discussed, including removal of material terms and a much reduced price that

Mukuru rationalized by citing the integration between our Malawi and Cape Town teams. It also specified several steps still remaining, which meant it would take us months to close even if we dropped everything else and pushed as hard as we could to address them.

I was furious. We should have better anticipated this move, especially after the pressure caused by their first offer. I now regretted granting the extension, which cost us a critical two weeks.

I scheduled an emergency board call to discuss our options. The positive dialog from our recent board meeting was displaced by an emotional and realistic fear of losing everything. Through the fog, three options emerged.

First, we could just shut down our Malawi business and drag Mukuru down with us. That risked destroying our agents as well as our relationships with other stakeholders in the Malawi market, including the Reserve Bank of Malawi. If we did this, we figured Mukuru would just sign up all of our agents onto their platform, taking a bit of pain in the short term but effectively getting what they wanted without having to buy us out with cash. We quickly ruled this out as a feasible option.

Second, we could try to find another buyer as fast as possible, as our term sheet exclusivity with Mukuru had now ended. It was doubtful anyone could move quickly enough, though; this would only be possible with a new injection of cash from shareholders, which was contingent on the Malawi sale that was now, ironically, in jeopardy. None of our shareholders wanted to step up, at least on their own, which also eliminated this option.

Or third, we could take an aggressive posture by breaking our partnership exclusivity and opening up our network to provide cash-out to Mukuru's competitors. Mukuru would likely seek a legal injunction to enforce an exclusivity clause we had in our contract, but we had consulted our lawyers and were encouraged that we had a strong legal position. The problem with this option was that Mukuru could just choose to withhold payment until any legal case was settled, which would bankrupt us instantly unless our shareholders were again willing to put in enough cash to buffer us and survive a prolonged legal fight.

In reality, without a miraculous quick injection of cash, we appeared to have no options.

To add salt to the wound — and taking a page out of the MNO playbook — Mukuru suddenly rolled out more than 30 of their own kiosks right next to ours in premium locations across Malawi. It's a good thing we hadn't gone for the first option and switched off our system, as our agents would have just moved into the Mukuru kiosks next door and we would have lost everything with nothing in return.

With our backs against the wall and cash flow dwindling, however, we were still not to be counted out. Brad came up with the creative idea of going back to Mukuru with an offer to sell them a narrow copy of our agent management code, which would be sufficient for our Malawi agents to transact on, and would include our flagship Zoona Cash float financing product. This would be of more value to Mukuru than us since we were betting for the future on our Tachyon platform, which we had yet to roll out in Malawi. If Mukuru would make the offer binding, we would take the cash and walk away from Malawi completely, even for B2B partnerships. I proposed this to Mukuru and they came back to the table a few days later with an upward price adjustment; it was still well below our original term sheet, but they agreed to make their offer fully binding.

This was the best we could do given the circumstances, but it still didn't solve our short-term cash-flow problem. We were going to run out of cash within weeks, and it was now clear that closing the Mukuru deal would take months — they would have to decouple the platform code they were buying and run a new due diligence — with no hope of a down payment. The change of events had also shifted the calculus for both our shareholders and lenders. There was now a significantly smaller pot to share, and MicroVest remained resolute that they wanted a partial principal repayment. Our shareholders were reluctant to put in more cash if a large proportion of the Mukuru proceeds were going to repay our lenders, which would leave us no further ahead from a cash perspective. Plus, we still had the $7.5-million overhang of convertible debt that was due to mature in a few months, not to mention $19-million of sunk Series A and Series B equity.

As this back-and-forth exchange between our shareholders and lenders played out behind the scenes, we stopped paying our rent and deferred payroll taxes with penalties to preserve cash. The amazing Zoona culture that we had nurtured and maintained for so many years was all but dead. Our staff who remained had stopped even asking about the Mukuru sale, expecting an LGT repeat. I started to imagine what it would mean for our agents, consumers, staff and me personally if we actually ran out of cash. I had drained my savings following a voluntary salary cut after our Series C collapsed, and Isabelle was now asking me if we might lose our house. I had operated on the margin for so long and had always found a way to regroup, but this time was different.

The end of my ten-year Zoona journey was upon me.

Exit Time

After a mentoring call with Patrick Pichette to seek advice on our predicament, I concluded that I only had one move left. On Monday, March 11, 2019 I told Brad and Brett that my time had come. I scheduled an emergency board call, preceded by a cover email that outlined my plan: By the end of the week, I was going to lay off our entire Cape Town team, except a few critical people to keep our system and call center running. I would hand over the CEO reins to Brad, but Brett and his team would also leave. By shedding all of our Cape Town people costs, we could try to turn the business cash-flow positive with the revenue from Zambia and Malawi. We couldn't afford to pay any severances but we could create a liability — which would get in line behind all of our other liabilities — in the hope that the affected staff would get something one day. I didn't know any of the legalities involved, but it was the only way I could see us surviving without an immediate agreement that brought new cash into the business.

Then came that most somber board call of my career, with many tears shed. My plan was received as well-intentioned, but in considering it our equity investors clearly realized that if Zoona were to become cash-flow positive at some point, our lenders would be able to take control of the business and render everyone's equity worthless. This finally forced their hand to step up and break through the bottleneck.

In the following days, a flurry of activity ensued. Three of our shareholders — Omidyar Network, Accion and Lundin — agreed in principle to invest more capital, but they needed assurance that there was still a future upside in the business from our new B2B strategy. For that to happen, Brett and his B2B team needed to stay, but we would still cut all non-essential roles. Also, our lenders, MicroVest and Blue Haven, would have to restructure their loans, converting a portion into equity and giving us a grace period on interest and principal payments. The shareholders, lenders and management would also need to agree on how much of the Mukuru money would be needed to run the business and get to profitability as quickly as possible. With me stepping out of the way, everyone got to work.

By making the call to exit, I had mobilized our shareholders, lenders and management to come together and jointly find a solution. If only I had had the courage to do this earlier, and so give everyone more time to work out the details and build in more negotiating leverage with Mukuru...

We did our best to keep the worst news from spreading among our staff. But they knew. They saw the emotions on our faces when we left meetings in the boardroom (which we had named the "partnership room" years before, when we believed the partnerships with our investors would lead to great success). And they saw the investors in our offices who had flown in on a moment's notice to discuss the intricacies of navigating the road ahead. And no doubt they saw how I avoided eye contact as I walked through our increasingly empty offices. By now the downstairs call center was vacant, with everyone consolidated upstairs as we attempted to sublet some of our unused space. And even though the back half of our offices was fenced off by potted plants, this still left an enormous open space in front, with just one or two people working at tables built for eight. The historic Cape Town building we had once envisioned as the headquarters for hundreds of Zoona employees was now a somber, cavernous place; its silence stood in stark contrast to the colorful signs and inspirational quotes that proclaimed our culture and values in every corner.

On April 1, 2019 — that deeply ironic anniversary — we assembled who we could on the bleachers we had installed in our Cape Town office for all-hands meetings. As many as 155 staff members had worked in this room not too long before, with an additional 75 in other offices; there were now just 83 people left in Cape Town (and 44 abroad). About half appeared, the others absent or attending to customer calls. Across from the bleachers, carved in wood, were the "Wildly Important Goals" we had created to guide Zoona to a very different future. It was the room where, so many times, I had announced — to much larger gatherings — our positive milestones for consumers, agents, revenue, investments and expansions, all to cheers and celebration. Even when I had much less heartening news, the vibe had still been positive.

Not this time.

I told everyone I was leaving. Then I announced that most of them would also be losing their jobs. Only the positions deemed essential to Zoona's B2B future would be retained as per the agreement reached between Brad and Brett, the shareholders and the lenders who were willing to continue supporting the company. As a small consolation, I was fortunate to hand over the CEO reins to Brad, my co-founder and longtime partner, who I knew would do a great job leading the necessary restructuring to keep Zoona alive while Brett focused on gaining traction with our B2B pivot.

There was no shock. There were no tears, as there had been when I announced Keith's departure. There was, in fact, almost a sense of relief. The uncertainty was dispelled, and it was clear that the main concern on everyone's mind was their own severance package and next steps, and not Zoona or me.

What was next, I had no idea. I just knew that I had failed to win.

EMBRACING FAILURE: WHAT I LEARNED

I made a few critical mistakes following the collapse of our Series C round.

First, I should have taken my final act, the decision to leave, earlier. The right moment of crisis to make foundational and leadership changes was right after our Series C collapsed. At the time I was overly emotional and trying to hang on against the odds, thinking we could find a new lead investor — this effectively deferred making a very hard decision. Had I instead resigned and handed over to Brad then, we could have cut deeper, pivoted faster and forced our debt and equity restructuring sooner. We could have still chosen to sell Zoona Malawi, but from a less precarious negotiating position, when we weren't racing toward a cliff. This all happened six months later, at a point when we had no alternative. It is the job of a leader to mobilize others to take actions they would otherwise not take on their own, and in this aspect I failed for too long and until it was very nearly too late.

Having failed to see this path at the time, I definitely should have taken it three months later upon receiving the first Mukuru offer and confirming that our shareholders had no intent to invest more cash into the business. We had bet everything on converting a non-binding pressure offer into a closed sale of Zoona Malawi within a very short time period, knowing we faced disaster if anything went wrong. I recognized at the time that this was risky and a recipe to get squeezed by Mukuru, but I didn't pull the emergency cord hard enough; instead, I put on my blinkers and hoped for the best. Hope should never become the strategy.

Looking further back, there is also a good argument that we should have sold Zoona Zambia on the way up or at the top of the S-curve. There were two missed opportunities to take this path. First, we could have done this after the Zambia currency crisis instead of raising a Series B investment and trying to expand, which was the start of many of our troubles. Second, we could have pursued an exit after our Mozambique failure rather than trying to raise a Series C; Zoona Zambia was still strong at the time but there were warning signs that the market was shifting toward mobile money. Instead, we made an implicit bet that we could raise a major round of capital from a weak position in a small market to fight against big MNO competitors.

What I failed to see at the time is that there was a path to sell our Zambia (and Malawi) subsidiaries *while retaining our team and technology*. My frame of reference was that an "exit" meant a total sale and the end of Zoona. I now see how we could have harvested cash from selling our subsidiaries (using some of it to pay down debt and possibly return some cash to shareholders), preserved our equity in our holding company that owned our technology and IP, and started again with our core team intact and years of acquired wisdom. This would have been a great position from which to redesign a new fintech strategy that leveraged our technology and considered how to enter other markets without a full replication of our Zambia model, which failed in Mozambique.

There was one other alternative outcome. I personally could have exited and handed the keys back to Brad and Brett much earlier. I had accomplished what I originally set out to do when I moved back to Zambia in 2009, by finding Brad and Brett, attracting international investment, and helping to scale Zoona up into a formidable and (before the Zambia currency crisis) profitable business. We all grew tremendously together, and both Brad and Brett were more than capable of being CEO; indeed, Brad's and my roles had probably overlapped too much and too often. I could have handed over to them at several points from positions of stability, or following crises when there was opportunity for change. It was always my belief and drive that we could keep raising larger investment rounds and chase a greater vision — and this was ultimately our undoing. Had I not been at the helm in the latter years, the business structure might have looked quite different, to everyone's ultimate benefit.

It's easy with hindsight to hypothesize how any of these alternative scenarios could have led to a better outcome than what happened at the end of my Zoona story — but they also might not have. The hard part about making strategic decisions about the future is that you don't know how the future is going to play out until it does. The one thing I know for certain is that, despite all of my mistakes and failings, I always did the best I could with the knowledge and capabilities I had at the time. I have no regrets — only gratitude for being part of the journey and having the opportunity to start a new one.

PART 3: WINNING

"Ever tried?
Ever failed?
No matter.
Try again.
Fail again.
Fail better."
– SAMUEL BECKETT

CHAPTER 11

EMBRACING AND LEARNING FROM FAILURE

In September 2018, with my confidence at an all-time low after Zoona's Series C had fallen apart, I was invited to New York to receive a prestigious award as one of the Schwab Foundation's 2018 Social Entrepreneurs of the Year. The last thing in the world I felt I deserved was an award, and I couldn't decide whether or not to attend the ceremony. My partners, Arjuna and Isabelle, eventually convinced me to get on the plane.

The main event was a closed-door dinner in honor of the awardees, with numerous luminaries in attendance: Queen Mathilde of Belgium, former U.S. Vice President Al Gore, World Bank President Jim Kim and Alibaba founder Jack Ma, among others, were there. At dinner, I was seated next to Christine Lagarde, managing director of the International Monetary Fund, who curiously enquired, "Tell me, how has it been to have the IFC as an investor?" We had a nice chat.

The star turnout may have been impressive, but the greatest impact on me was a facilitated session on well-being with current and past Schwab awardees. We were presented with data on the high probability of entrepreneurs experiencing depression, especially during times of failure. When the facilitator listed the symptoms, I ticked off every single one in my head, and as I looked around the room I saw everyone else nodding along as well. He then led us through a twenty-minute group meditation focused on identifying and reaching out to our "inner critic" — that voice inside our head, which we all have, that conflates "you failed" with "you're a failure." There is a critical difference between these two messages, and if you can learn to hear the former and block out the latter, you allow yourself an opportunity for growth.

It took me a long while and a lot of external support to believe this, as I very much felt like a failure. After announcing my exit to our staff, I travelled to Oxford in April 2019 to attend the annual summit of past and present Skoll Scholars, preceding the much larger Skoll World Forum for Social Entrepreneurship. Some forty of us Skollars made the pilgrimage from around the world to reconnect and create a safe and closed community of support.

It was only fitting that I volunteered, as I had done in 2017, to speak at "Fuck-Up Night," where attendees present their stories of failure. I was given ten minutes, but I spoke for more than an hour to a captivated audience. It was an intensely emotional experience, and when I finished I was surrounded by fellow Skollars coming up to hug me. One of them suggested I write my story down so that others might learn from it.

Immediately afterwards, I was invited to speak at the public "Fail Faire" as a side event to the main Skoll World Forum, which spilled into many more conversations over drinks and coffee until my voice was completely hoarse. My story was still very raw and intensely emotional as it poured out of me. I felt the support of so many people, including other entrepreneurs who seemed to resonate with every word, and it was immensely reaffirming to feel that I was not alone.

I flew back to Cape Town, and for the rest of the month worked side by side with Brad to hand things over to him, though there wasn't actually much for me to do. There were board and leadership meetings happening and, for the first time, I wasn't part of them. I filled my remaining days sending personal emails to everyone in my network notifying them of my exit and thanking them for all their support over the years. It was amazing and humbling to realize how many people had contributed to making Zoona what it was — and who had contributed to making me who I am.

On the last Friday of the month, as was traditional, we gathered staff into the common room to say goodbye to anyone leaving the company. These had always had an air of celebration, but this time just a scattering of people were there, some of whom would be toasted and sent off at the next Friday gathering. Brett played a tribute video about my time at Zoona that Sevie — the videographer who had accompanied me on my customer immersion trip — had put together. I smiled and had a drink, but I couldn't help thinking that this wasn't how I had envisioned my Zoona story ending a decade earlier.

Isabelle arrived to pick me up. She didn't want to come upstairs, but I cajoled her to join us to at least say hello. I shook a few hands. Then we headed for the elevator and watched the door close on this chapter of our lives.

Self-Discovery

I had more than one crisis of confidence in the days and weeks after leaving Zoona. As my email traffic ground to a halt, my mind immediately jumped to "What's next?" — exacerbated by the many well-meaning questions everyone was asking me. I grew envious of positive LinkedIn updates and announcements of startup funding rounds. My identity had been so tied up as the CEO of Zoona that for the first time in years I felt lost and empty without a company to build or a team to lead.

There was also the challenge of money. I had long ago paid back my parents the $100,000 they loaned me in 2010, and I left with a standard severance package from Zoona, but much of it was at risk until the Malawi sale closed (which ended up finally happening a full year later). The thought of having to jump into consulting or get a "real job" terrified me more than anything else. I was the very definition of burnt out.

In early May 2019 I had coffee with Karl Westvig, a South African fintech CEO I admired who had gone through a similar transition in the past. He gave me the sensible advice to take a break and focus on healing. At that point, I couldn't stop talking or thinking about Zoona from morning to night. Even my sleep was still broken and anxious. I had to give myself time and space to put Zoona behind me and clear my head. He also advised me to take a leap of faith and not worry about money; if things got tight, Karl offered to find something for me to do at his company, which was both very kind and greatly appreciated.

Nevertheless, Isabelle and I started making plans to tighten our belts and rent our house while I embraced the notion of taking a break. I started meditating and went on long solo hikes and mountain bike rides. I spent more time with my kids and just tried to *be* for a while. It was a dramatic change of pace, but one I started to enjoy as the fog slowly lifted.

Several weeks later, I was fortunate to attend an executive leadership course at Harvard, also supported by the Schwab Foundation, with forty other leading social entrepreneurs from around the world. I wasn't nearly ready to re-engage, but

I found it to be an amazing opportunity for reflection among an inspiring and supportive group. I also learned a fitting definition of leadership from one of the lecturers, Tim O'Brien: Leadership is the act of mobilizing others to confront and make progress on a difficult reality they would rather avoid.

For the first time, I reflected on the emergency board meeting I had called to announce my departure along with all of our staff — which triggered our shareholders and lenders to come together to find a solution — and saw it as one of my best leadership moments, even though it was my final one. Patrick Pichette had called me to tell me as much at the time, but through my emotion I hadn't taken his words on board. Now I understood, and I held my head a bit higher.

At Harvard, I was challenged to create my "story of self" — to go way back to my childhood and formative years to figure out what had shaped my values and started me on the path to becoming who I am today. Growing up in Calgary, Canada, I had never imagined myself ending up as a purpose-driven fintech entrepreneur in Africa. How and why did this happen?

I started writing. I wrote about my childhood and school years, and the influence of my parents on establishing my values and modeling leadership, hard work and gender equity. I wrote about the joy I experienced after discovering Engineers Without Borders at university, and my subsequent experiences immersing myself in the local culture while volunteering in Ghana and Zambia. I wrote about my leap to attend the London School of Economics, a place where I met my wife Isabelle, to study why and how some countries grew rich while others became or stayed poor. I wrote about getting my lucky break to pursue an MBA at Oxford's Saïd Business School as a Skoll Scholar for Social Entrepreneurship, where I came up with the idea to start African Enterprise Partners to connect impact investors with purpose-driven African entrepreneurs building scalable companies. And then I wrote about Mobile Transactions and how it evolved to become Zoona.

As I wrote, I started to realize that in between the failures, there was a lot of winning. Between launching our first champion agent on Cairo Road in Lusaka in April 2009 and my leaving in April 2019, Zoona processed $2.5-billion in transactions for millions of previously underserved consumers. More than 3,000 people gained the opportunity to run their own businesses and serve their communities as Zoona agents and tellers. And for our effort we earned $86-million in revenue, proving that a purpose-driven business in a small African market can also be a viable one.

Zoona played a catalyzing role in shaping the markets and laying the foundations for financial inclusion in Zambia and Malawi, and of that I am tremendously proud. In 2019, the UN Capital Development Fund and the Bank of Zambia recorded more than 6.5 million active consumer digital financial services accounts, 90,000 active agents and a 56 percent growth in annual transactions in Zambia[2]. The Finscope 2020 Zambia survey highlighted how financial inclusion, measured as access and informed usage of both formal and informal financial service products, increased from 37.4 percent in 2009 to 69.4 percent in 2020 in Zambia[3]. The trends in Malawi are similar, and remittances (primarily from South Africa and cashed out at former Zoona agents) accounted for approximately 2.4 percent of the country's GDP

---

2 *State of the Digital Financial Services Market in Zambia 2019 — Results from the UNCDF Annual Provider Survey* (UNCDF); available at uncdf.org

3 *Finscope 2020: Top Line Findings* (Finscope); available at www.fsdzambia.org

in 2019[4]. These two relatively small and previously obscure markets are in the midst of a digital transformation and are better off because of Zoona.

We were also pioneers in Africa's emerging startup ecosystem. The more than $35-million in equity, debt and grant capital we raised was at the leading edge of a wave that saw $2-billion raised in 250 investment rounds in 2019, according to the Partech Africa annual report[5] — with a huge focus on fintech. The report only starts tracking funding rounds from 2015, six years after we raised our first seed investment from the Grassroots Business Fund, and three years after our Series A. I am immensely proud of the role we played in setting an example for purpose-driven entrepreneurs in Africa, and making it easier for them to secure the capital they need from international investors.

Writing helped me to realize that no matter the outcome, Zoona mattered. We laid the foundations upon which others built. When I finished, I had a 120,000-word "letter to my therapist," and I felt much better. It was time to get moving again and start a new journey.

Re-Start

In September 2019, the Skoll Centre for Social Entrepreneurship at Oxford invited me to be a Social Entrepreneur in Residence to start answering the question "What's next?" By that point I already knew. Writing had turned a pilot light into a flame to do it all over again — but differently.

I started by creating a "Me on a Page" document that clarified

---

4 *Malawi Financial Inclusion Refresh* (UNCDF); available at uncdf.org
5 *2019 Africa Tech Venture Capital Report* (Partech Africa Team);
   available at partechpartners.com

my personal values and succinctly answered a few fundamental questions:

Why do I exist?

I am a privileged entrepreneur at my core. I have a responsibility to take on hard global challenges in order to relieve the systemic suffering of others while finding peace and joy for myself.

What big problem am I inspired to tackle for the next ten years?

I believe that micro-, small and medium enterprises (MSMEs) are a critically important pillar of economic development and sustainable job creation in emerging economies. Without support to join and benefit from the digital economy, they risk being left behind, which will contribute to growing inequality and other social challenges.

How can I best contribute?

I believe the best way I can contribute to addressing this challenge is by building tech-enabled companies that exist to release the core pain points of MSME customers, infused with purpose and designed to scale.

I got to work to design a new venture that I called "Boost," with the ten-year goal of enabling ten million MSMEs to be included — and thrive — in Africa's emerging digital economy in order to create sustainable jobs and income. I put together a structure and business model that drew directly from lessons learned from my biggest past failures, and that was designed (in contrast to Zoona) to be multi-market from day one.

I teamed up with three co-founders I had worked with at Zoona — Joseph Kuvor, Isaac Aidoo and Du Toit Marais — to test it in Ghana and South Africa.

We first piloted it with a handful of informal women-owned grocery stores in Accra, who ordered stock by WhatsApping us lists of the products they needed, which Isaac would buy from the central market and deliver to them, saving them time and hassle as a starting value proposition. A few months later in South Africa, I connected Du Toit to the informal sector guru GG Alcock. He in turn recruited an accomplished entrepreneur in the food sector, Nontwenle Mchunu, and they applied this same concept to informal fast-food restaurants in townships that ordered order meat and other fresh goods. In both countries, we planned to boost our customers with stock advances to help them grow and ultimately create sustainable jobs and income.

Also in contrast to Zoona, I wanted each Boost company to be *owned and run* by the local founding entrepreneurs who shared my passion for enabling MSMEs, and who were experienced business builders themselves. They would trade as independent Boost-branded franchises, but leverage a shared technology, brand and operations backbone. They also wouldn't have to worry about spending all of their time chasing investors; as much as I didn't enjoy the later stage fundraising at Zoona, I realized that I had developed a strong capital-raising skill set and network that could be of service to Boost franchise founders, so that they could stay focused on the real work of acquiring and serving their customers. This time, though, I would ensure that only mission-aligned, value-adding and supportive long-term investors would get a seat on the Boost bus. I would also push hard to get each Boost franchise to profitability as efficiently as possible to minimize our dependence on that next investment round.

I put this all into an investment deck and started pitching again. I thought enough time had passed that raising seed funding to start again wouldn't be very difficult, especially as this time I had a track record. Many investors I knew well were interested, but I experienced dozens upon dozens of rejections for the first five months for any variety of cited reasons. It seemed that because of my Zoona track record, investors were willing to give me the opportunity to pitch my idea in full and engage in weeks of conversations, but they weren't prepared to back it until I reached the same level of traction they were accustomed to from first-time entrepreneurs. This was an important learning for me, and differed from the stories I'd heard of repeat Silicon Valley entrepreneurs who could seemingly raise big seed rounds purely on reputation. In the fledgling African startup ecosystem, I didn't find this true and had to start at the beginning with everyone else.

And then Covid-19 hit. In March 2020, I found myself working from the small annex of my house, with toys scattered all over the floor and my two kids sharing a room and double bed because we had rented our house for the Cape Town summer to cover my missing income. I still had no funding for Boost and almost no investor leads and, with the pandemic upon us, now no ability to travel. My personal cash runway was dropping in contrast to my rising stress levels as South Africa prepared to close schools and enter into one of the hardest lockdowns in the world.

But I had learned from my past that it takes only one spark to start a fire. Almost every opportunity comes from one timely introduction, phone call or pitch. This one came with an introduction from an entrepreneur I was mentoring in Uganda, who linked me to a Japanese seed investor in Africa I didn't previously know: Kepple Ventures. Rather than waiting out Covid, Kepple leaned in after one phone call and wired the first $100,000 into my newly formed Boost business bank account in early April 2020. I kept refreshing my account balance screen over and over again to make sure the money was real. It was.

That was the spark. The pilot light lit when my longtime Canadian friend Mary Roach, who had been the very first overseas volunteer with Engineers Without Borders two decades earlier, took the plunge to join as my co-founder. Mary was based in London and had built a career in operations, much of it in Africa, building and investing in tech-enabled companies. We shared the same values and philosophy, and her strengths matched the weaknesses that had plagued me all throughout my Zoona journey. Mary was excited by Boost's vision and model, and the Kepple funding provided the comfort she needed to start.

Since neither of us could build technology, we needed a technical co-founder. I sent an email to my network with a role profile, and almost instantly I was referred to Will Croft. Will was also based in London and coincidentally had overlapped with Mary for a few years at another organization. Covid had also disrupted the data startup that Will had co-founded, and after a few conversations he dove in headfirst to write Boost's first lines of code at the end of April. Out of all my entrepreneurial achievements, sourcing and closing the elusive technical co-founder in two weeks is one of my best!

My parents took advantage of plunging Canadian bank interest rates to once again help me with some bridge financing, and when the Zoona Malawi sale closed, triggering my final severance payment, I finally had some personal breathing room. Between May and August, Mary, Will and I raised a further $370,000 in pre-seed investment from a set of Boost backers, including Patrick Pichette, who I was grateful to have on board again. To my surprise, I didn't know most of our early investors — they came through warm introductions from people I reached out to and even spontaneously from people who had simply heard I was starting something and thought I might like to be connected to a prospective investor. This was another important learning for me: I had a decent investor network from Zoona, but the early stage and angel investors I needed for Boost were one step removed and dispersed around the world; I had to go through weak network ties to access them. When I did, my Zoona track record spoke for itself, and they backed me quickly and without much hassle.

From the beginning, I designed Boost's structure and model to be as lean and asset-light as possible, with everyone able to work remotely and without the need for a head office. But I didn't anticipate just how apt it would be in a Covid (and also post-Covid) world. Over the next several months, without visiting any of these markets, we gained traction in Ghana and South Africa, and then recruited co-founders to set up and launch a Boost franchise in Nigeria. When Isabelle got a new job, our family packed up and moved to London in December 2020, which was a good excuse for me to meet Will for the very first time and be closer to him and Mary. Never mind that after we arrived, London went into a national lockdown and I only managed to physically see them once in my first four months...

While it was not without challenges, what made Boost's start possible was a relentless focus on choosing the fewest *right* people and designing the culture we wanted from the very beginning. We did this by creating a set of virtues (non-negotiable, action-oriented values) and principles (general rules and algorithms designed to efficiently achieve our goals) that are meant to build a shared way of working across all Boost teams in different markets, even though they may never meet each other. Already, I have seen how these virtues and principles have enabled us to start from a place that took us years of failing to get to at Zoona. I hope that they can also help you embrace the notion of failing to win in your life and entrepreneurial journey, whatever that may be.

VIRTUES — TO LIVE BY

Be purpose-driven: Define your purpose and make it the focal point for everything you do.

Be tenacious: Embrace the struggle of entrepreneurship, and fight through adversity as and when it comes.

Be compassionate: Put yourself in the shoes of others to empathize with their perspectives and pain points, and then take action to make things better for them.

Be whole: You can love your work, but you are more than your work; prioritize your mental, emotional, physical and spiritual well-being.

Be good: Always take the high road and do the right thing, even in the face of temptation.

TEAM PRINCIPLES — TO BUILD A GREAT CULTURE

Know yourself and others: Becoming a high-performing team starts with hyper-awareness of the individual strengths and weaknesses, personality preferences and underlying motivations of yourself and your teammates.

Listen by default: To achieve deep understanding, pass the microphone and listen to what others are saying, even when they are not speaking.

Employ respectful candor: Always speak your truth, even when it hurts — but do so respectfully and mindfully to minimize the noise surrounding your messages.

Assume good intent: Start by acknowledging that positions you disagree with or don't understand come from the same good place as your own.

Debate, decide and commit FAST: Engage in rigorous debate, but even when the outcome is uncertain, make a decision, get behind it and move forward.

In God we trust; everyone else must bring data: It's OK to have strong opinions, but they should be backed up by data and open to change.

Hypothesize and test before building: Before sinking resources and committing to a path, design a hypothesis and ask, "How might we test it?"

Embrace and learn from failure: *Failure comes hand in hand with taking risks, so when it happens accept it, grieve and reflect on what you will do differently next time.*

Celebrate milestones: *When milestones are achieved, no matter how small or seemingly insignificant, ring the bell and celebrate.*

Do your best work: *Something is only done when you can honestly say it is the best you can do.*

BUSINESS PRINCIPLES — TO BUILD CAPABILITIES TO WIN

Put your core customers first: *Understand who your core customers are, and do the things that solve their pain points and delight them.*

Build with only the fewest right people: *Resist hiring too far ahead of the curve, and build small teams with highly capable people who are motivated by your purpose and fit your culture.*

Stay digital-led, tech-enabled and asset-light: *Design scalable models that are capital-efficient, but never forget that people live in a physical world and are resistant to change.*

Enable the entrepreneurs: *Outsource problems to passionate and experienced entrepreneurs with skin in the game, and remove their constraints to growth.*

Design for scale: *Start small but think big, and create a thoughtful roadmap with multiple options to get to the end goal.*

Scale with positive unit economics: *Making money at scale requires first understanding and proving how to make money from a single customer.*

Build a branded community: *Go deeper than just transactional relationships with your customers and stakeholders by creating a community anchored by your brand.*

Invest in your core: *Avoid being over-excited by new and shiny initiatives, and ensure that your core is well-defined and sufficiently resourced.*

Lead your customers before your competitors do: Don't underestimate your future competitors and never stop innovating to find better solutions for your customers.

Don't run out of cash: The best team with the best culture with the best product only wins if it has enough cash to compete.

ENDNOTE & GRATITUDE

"Gratitude turns what we have into enough."
– AESOP

After I left Zoona, Brad and Brett Magrath kept the company afloat by slimming down the team, completing a cap table restructuring, closing the Malawi sale, and turning Zoona into an interoperable cash-in cash-out agent network in Zambia that served even MTN Money. Brad stepped down as CEO a year later to start a new chapter mentoring African entrepreneurs. He handed the baton to Brett, who in parallel was bringing his B2B fintech vision to life under a new brand called Tilt. I have remained in contact with them and with Keith Davies, who became an even closer friend once I was no longer his boss! I'm grateful to all three of them, for a decade of fellowship and for teaching me how to be an entrepreneur and a partner.

I'm grateful to my parents, Susan and Don Quinn, for instilling my foundational values and sense of purpose, and for believing in me enough to take the financial risk that made my entrepreneurial journey possible. I always felt your unwavering love and support, even half a world apart and during my periods of peak stress.

I'm grateful to Patrick Pichette, for being my backer and mentor throughout my journey, and for always giving me sound and honest advice — especially when I didn't want to hear it.

I'm grateful to Arjuna Costa and Monica Brand-Engel, for backing Zoona early and for being exemplary investors, even through the hard times.

I'm grateful to everyone who worked at Zoona, to our agents who took risks with us and to our consumers who trusted us.

I'm grateful to all of our board members, investors, partners and advisors who backed us, encouraged us and guided us.

I'm grateful to the rest of my and Isabelle's family for their support despite the distance — Erin, Dave, Rylan, Rowan, Meriel, Carlo, David and Lorenzo.

I'm grateful to my Boost community for believing in me and joining me on a new journey — Mary, Will, Julia, Joseph, Isaac, Augustine, Du Toit, GG, Nonts, Peter, Koye, Ndidi and Benedikt, and all of our backers, partners and employees.

I'm especially grateful to my wife Isabelle, for riding the entire rollercoaster with me and always giving me unflagging support, encouragement and love, even when I was physically and emotionally absent. And to Aurelia and Lucca for their patience and love throughout — you are my reason for being. Daddy finally finished his book!

This book would not have been possible without support and contributions from the following people:

Adrian Dommisse, Alex Lazarow, Brad Magrath, Brett Magrath, Brian Requarth, Don Quinn, Elizabeth Filippouli, Elizabeth Rossiello, Elizabeth Yin, Fred Swaniker, Katlego Maphai, GG Alcock, Keith Davies, Marc Ventresca, Marlon Parker, Matt Flannery, Michael Jordaan, Dr Ndidi Nnoli-Edozien, Nikhil

Dugal, Patrick and Tamar Pichette, Dr Rutendo Hwindingwi, Thomas Hellmann and everyone else who read through various versions and always offered valuable advice — especially Susan Quinn.

My platinum crowdfunding backers: BFA Global Catalyst Fund, Engineers Without Borders Canada, Marc Ventresca and Oxford Saïd Business School.

My gold crowdfunding backers: Ademola Adesina, Anna Eliasson, Daniel Ball, Don and Susan Quinn, Financial Sector Deepening Mozambique, Gagan Biyani, Marjolijn Dijksterhuis, Meriel and Carlo Carboni, Michael Schlein, Namukaba Hichilo, Patrick and Tamar Pichette, Susan Phillips and William De Laslow.

My silver crowdfunding backers: Alexandros Germanis, Anca Bogdana Rusu, Angus Brown, Benjamin Knelman, Brendan Baker, Dale Weaver, David and Robin Damberger, Ernest Darkoh, Eugene Amusin, Feven Habtom, Fiona Macaulay, Gail Damberger, George Bevis, Henry Gonzalez, Howard Chen, Jane Scowcroft, Janine Firpo, Johan Bosini, John Bazley, John Lazar, Joseph Kuvor, Katlego Maphai, Khalid Al Kharusi, Llew Claasen, Louis Dorval, Maelis Carraro, Mariah Hartman, Marian Wentworth, Matthew Farmer, Michael Anderson, Michael Starkenburg, Pradeep Suthram, Richard Webb, Robel Chiappini, Shane Etzenhouser and Brukty Tigabu, Steven Moore, Sunil Goyal, Suzanne Skees, Tie Mudge, Tom Anderson, and Tom and Amanda Robinson.

My bronze crowdfunding backers.

ENDNOTE & GRATITUDE

My editors Lisa Raleigh, Rory O'Connor and Tim Richman; my designer Sean Robertson; Ania Rokita, Deb Rudman and the team at Burnet Media; and the team at The Audiobook Producers in London.

Everyone else who contributed financially, in kind or in spirit!

PICTURE CAPTIONS

Part 1 opener (p18)
Zoona's first champion agent outlet, on Lusaka's Cairo Road, with the post office looming in the background. The outlet was established in 2009, but this picture was taken nearly a decade, and countless transactions, later.

Part 2 opener (p70)
Mercy (kiosk on left) serving consumers in Ndola, Zambia next to competing MTN and Airtel kiosks, 2017.

Part 3 opener (p260)
Mike presenting Zoona's TED-style talk for the Girl Effect Accelerator at the San Francisco Palace of Fine Arts, 2014.

Over the page
Just doing business. Mike and Memory in Lilongwe, Malawi, 2017.

FAILING TO WIN

SEND MONEY HERE
NEW Geisha
with extracts from
mother nature
NO ONE
FASTER!
SEND MON
ND MONEY HERE

Keep in touch with Mike:

mikequinn.co

@mikepquinn

mikep-quinn

And follow Boost, his latest venture:

boost.technology

@withboost

boosttechnology

Printed in Great Britain
by Amazon